PROFILE
of the
Isle of Man

ISLE OF MAN BANK

a concise history

Lily Publications Ltd.,
PO Box 33, Ramsey, Isle of Man,
British Isles IM99 4LP

Tel: +44(0) 1624 898446
www.lilypublications.com

Derek Winterbottom

ISBN: 9781899602872

Produced and designed by Lily Publications Ltd
Printed and bound in Sweden.

© Lily Publications Ltd 2007

Published by Lily Publications Ltd
Registered office: PO Box 33, Ramsey, Isle of Man, IM7 3HD.
Tel: +44 (0)1624 898446
Fax: +44 (0)1624 898449
Email: info@lilypublications.co.uk
Web: www.lilypublications.co.uk

Title Page: *On the West Coast, looking towards Niarbyl. (Miles Cowsill)*

Contents

The mediaeval Monks' Bridge, Ballasalla. (Miles Cowsill)

Foreword

No history of the Island would be complete without reference to Isle of Man Bank itself which has been an integral part of the Manx community since 1865. For that reason we are pleased to be involved with a publication which traces the development of the Island over the centuries.

The publishers were faced with an awesome assignment in charting this progress but the same could equally be said of our legislators in the late 1950s and early 60s who had to turn around a depressed economy and find ways of boosting the local job market. Now, we not only offer a wide variety of careers to our young people but also welcome those from the UK, mainland Europe and beyond to fill the vacancies created in finance, technology and other industries – surely testimony to the fact that the mission was accomplished.

This metamorphosis into the well respected and successful finance centre of today was not achieved overnight but the Isle of Man is now a player on the world stage. In many respects the development of Isle of Man Bank mirrors that of the Island. At the end of its first year the Bank had made a profit of precisely £20 but has grown from an entirely local institution to one of international standing.

I suppose the lesson we must learn from history is that we should adapt constantly to changing circumstances. The quality of our workforce is what decides whether we can maintain economic growth, and if jobs should be lost in one sector we have to re-train and focus on another.

Throughout all the changes which are inevitable in any financial organisation Isle of Man Bank has never forgotten its roots. Our community investment programme has donated many thousands of pounds to activities ranging from the arts to sport; the majority of our staff are Manx, while support for local business initiatives is second-to-none. This is why I was delighted to be asked to write the foreword for this book and to wish the publishers every success.

Geoff Gelling
Head of Retail Banking
Isle of Man Bank

Isle of Man Bank, Douglas. (Miles Cowsill)

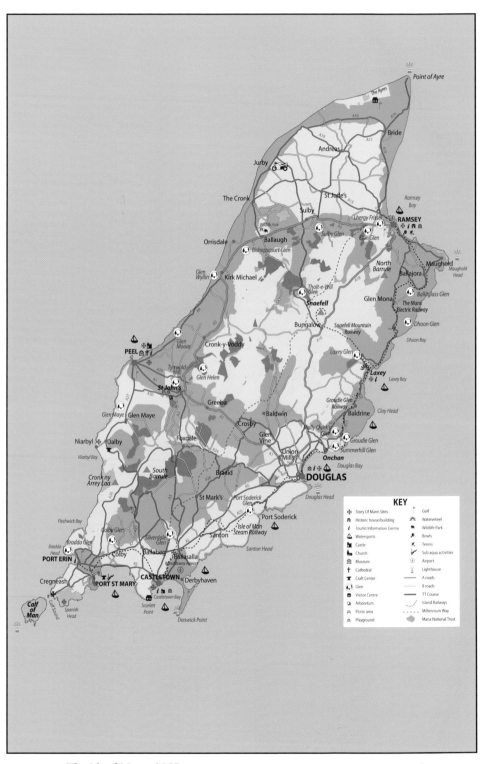

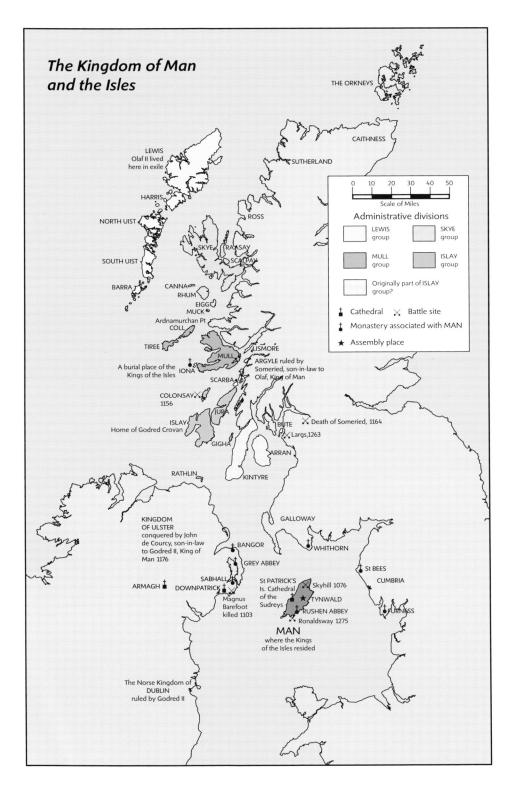

The Kingdom of Man and the Isles

THE ORKNEYS

CAITHNESS

SUTHERLAND

LEWIS
Olaf II lived
here in exile

HARRIS

NORTH UIST

ROSS

0 10 20 30 40 50

Scale of Miles

Administrative divisions

LEWIS group

SKYE group

MULL group

ISLAY group

Originally part of ISLAY group?

✝ Cathedral   ✗ Battle site

✝ Monastery associated with MAN

★ Assembly place

SKYE   RAASAY

SCALPAY

SOUTH UIST

BARRA

CANNA

RHUM

EIGG

MUCK

Ardnamurchan Pt

COLL

TIREE

MULL

LISMORE

A burial place of the
Kings of the Isles

IONA

ARGYLE ruled by
Someried, son-in-law to
Olaf, King of Man

SCARBA

COLONSAY
1156

JURA

ISLAY
Home of Godred Crovan

BUTE

✗ Death of Someried, 1164

✗ Largs,1263

GIGHA

ARRAN

RATHLIN

KINTYRE

GALLOWAY

KINGDOM
OF ULSTER
conquered by John
de Courcy, son-in-law
to Godred II, King of
Man 1176

✝ BANGOR

WHITHORN

GREY ABBEY

St BEES

SABHALL

ARMAGH

DOWNPATRICK

St PATRICK'S
Is. Cathedral
of the
Sudreys

Skyhill 1076

CUMBRIA

Magnus
Barefoot
killed 1103

TYNWALD ★

RUSHEN ABBEY

FURNESS

✗ Ronaldsway 1275

MAN
where the Kings
of the Isles resided

The Norse Kingdom of
DUBLIN
ruled by Godred II

9

Douglas c1830 by Joseph Strutt. (Manx National Heritage)

Preface

In this book I have attempted to provide an up-to-date short history of the Isle of Man, based on the latest available scholarship. I was fortunate to have access to three of the projected five volumes of A New History of the Isle of Man, the published versions of volumes one and five, and the page-proofs of volume three. The biggest gap to breach was the period from 1405 to 1830, a task which is proving formidable for the editors of the much-awaited volume four, which covers these years, and which proved both the most challenging and the most interesting for me.

I have listed my sources in the bibliography but this is a general history and I have not included footnotes. Although in the past the spelling Mann was often used as an alternative to Man, its usage is anachronistic today when the Island is officially designated the Isle of Man, so I have used that spelling throughout. In the mediaeval period, which is more fully covered in this book than in some short histories, I have used names derived from Latin, e.g. Godred and Reginald, rather than the Norse or Gaelic equivalents which were probably used at the time. I have also quoted the Chronicles of the Kings of Man and the Isles at some length, partly to emphasize how heavily we depend upon them for the medieval period and partly to bring the reader closer to this vital source. As I write this in the autumn of 2007 the original manuscript, hardly the size of this book, but very precious, is on a short loan from the British Library to the Manx Museum, where it is proudly on display.

Particular thanks are due to Roger Sims and his staff in the Manx National Heritage Library and also to the staff of the recently re-sited Henry Bloom Noble Library in Douglas which has an excellent local history section boasting fine views of the promenade. My publisher, Miles Cowsill, has taken many of the photographs which are a feature of the book, and we are both grateful to our sponsor the Isle of Man Bank. Above all, however, I would like to thank Peter Davey, who has just retired after a remarkably prolific and creative career as the first Director of Liverpool University's Centre for Manx Studies in Douglas. He generously gave me access to his draft overview of the Island's archaeological history and alerted me to the opinions of recent researchers, particularly in the prehistoric period, and I am very grateful for his time and support.

It is important to be realistic about the past. We might sometimes complain about the pressures and complexities of society today but generally we live a far easier, far longer and more secure life than our ancestors, most of whom had to struggle to survive. Note, just as one example, what proportion of people today wear spectacles and consider how hazy must have been the view of many before the advent of prescription lenses not very long ago. Constant advances in medical care and hygiene have greatly improved the quality and length of the average modern life, while rapid transport and successive revolutions in scientific research and electronic communication are still transforming our understanding of the world. With every new decade and its discoveries, the past becomes even less familiar and accessible. Yet we ignore the past at our peril because it alone explains the present, while a knowledge of our history gives us a chance to work out for ourselves who we are and in what direction we ought to be going.

Derek Winterbottom
October 2007

Castletown (Miles Cowsill)

St Michael's Island. (Miles Cowsill)

Chapter One
Foundations

EVOLUTION

Scientific research has led to the estimate that the Earth is about 4.6 billion years old. In the immensely long time span since then the planet has been through many drastic changes as its outer crust hardened and land masses and seas were formed, destroyed and formed again. The Earth's surface has been greatly affected by a series of vast tectonic plates which move very slowly below the outer crust. Some are on a collision course and when this happens, earthquakes and volcanoes result. Other plates are moving without hindrance and it has been calculated that the Atlantic Ocean is currently becoming wider at the rate of 50 millimetres a year. This does not sound much when measured in the span of a human lifetime but in a hundred million years, it will have widened by 5,000 kilometres.

The tectonic plate associated with the land mass from which the Isle of Man was eventually formed has moved north over the last 500 million years from cool regions of the southern hemisphere, where most of the Manx hills originate, across the equator and up towards its present position. The Castletown limestone, for instance, was probably formed at the equator about 330 million years 'BP' (before the present). Despite the age of the Earth most of the surviving rocks in the British Isles are less than 550 million years old. On the Isle of Man the oldest and most widespread rocks are of the Manx and Dalby groups, which were formed in the Lower Palaeozoic era, between about 450 to 420 million years BP. In addition, the Island has rocks from the Devonian period, about 50 million years later, and also the Carboniferous, which is the period to which the Castletown limestone belongs. Between about 290 and 206 BP, Permo-Triassic rocks were deposited but they lie underneath the Island's northern plain. Because the Island only broke away from the main British land mass at a very late stage its rocks are far from unique and the Manx and Dalby groups have much in common with rocks in the Lake District, southern Scotland and Leinster.

After the end of the Triassic period the embryo Isle of Man area experienced about two hundred million years of changes which have left no rocks preserved from this era, either because they were never deposited or because they have been destroyed by seismic convulsion or erosion. From a wider study of the Irish Sea region it can be assumed that during this period the area was steadily drifting northwards and it experienced significant climatic change, volcanic activity, erosion and tectonic subsidence. Evidence of volcanic activity is provided by solidified magma which can still be found in many of the Island's dykes and which dates from the Tertiary period, from about 65 million to about 4 million years BP.

It seems that the planet's temperature peaked about 55 million years BP and 20 million years later an ice cap formed over Antarctica. The Quaternary period, or 'Ice Age' began about 2.6 million years BP and during this period some 50 warm and cold cycles have been traced in various parts of the world. As far as the Island is concerned the earliest evidence of glaciation is at the Point of Ayre and it can be traced back at least 150,000 years, and perhaps much earlier. After this there was a long period when the region was probably free of ice, though still very cold. About 35,000 years ago ice advanced from what is now Scotland and covered the region, then withdrew. About 12,000 years later the ice came back and stopped roughly at what is now Bride before retreating. The last ice sheet returned about 16,000 years BP and stopped near what is now Jurby before retreating altogether about a thousand years later. It is sobering to reflect that, taking a long term view, many scientists argue that we are still in the middle of an Ice Age and sooner or later the ice will be back.

The chief legacy on the Island of the Ice Age is the Northern Plain, formed when the retreating ice left glacial debris piled up against the Snaefell mountain mass. The present coastal cliffs offer clear evidence of the glacial period, as do the Bride hills which are a glacial moraine. Geologists have recently concluded that

> Within its small area the Island displays a range of glacial phenomena barely matched elsewhere in Britain. In addition to almost every variety of glacial landform, including moraines, ice-front alluvial fans, outwash sandur, kettle holes and subglacial channel systems, it also has excellent exposure of almost every type of glacial deposit. Some of the largest and most complex glaciotectonic structures in Britain also occur, at Shellag Point. Added to these are excellent exposures of late and post-glacial organic sediments, both terrestrial and marine, containing a rich record of fossil fauna

17

Skeleton of the Giant Deer. (Manx National Heritage)

and flora including the Giant Deer. Also, beneath the northern plain, the Island records one of the thickest Quaternary depositional sequences in Britain, with glacial and interglacial deposits to at least 145m below sea level and a maximum thickness of the order of 250m. Much of the upper part of this thickness is exposed in the 25km of almost continuous cliff section bounding the northern plain and these sections exhibit ... a glacial sequence of such diverse character that it is probably unsurpassed in Britain.*

During the period of the Ice Age the Island region was probably populated with animals such as reindeer, elk, mountain hare, wolf,

* *Chiverrell and Thomas, p127 (See Sources, p216)*

lynx, arctic fox, and lemmings. There were also beetles, and study of their remains – found chiefly in the coastal cliffs of Jurby and in Glen Balleira – has been crucial in establishing some idea of the environment and climate in this period. The most spectacular animal that lived in this region was undoubtedly the Giant Deer, or Irish elk, a magnificent creature with antlers spanning 3.6 metres and which stood 2.1 metres at the shoulder. It appeared across northwestern Europe about 400,000 years BP, along with other 'megafauna' such as the woolly mammoth and sabre-toothed cat, and two notable examples have been found on the Island. The first was discovered in 1819 AD near Ballaugh and consisted of an almost complete and very well preserved skeleton which was reconstructed by a local blacksmith who then made a charge for people to see it. This came to the notice of the Governor of the Island, the Duke of Atholl, who used legal means to acquire it and presented it to the museum of the University of Edinburgh. Its existence was then proclaimed worldwide by the French naturalist George Cuvier, who described it in an influential book on bones and fossils. The skeleton of this animal is currently in the Royal Scottish Museum in Edinburgh and a portion of the antler has been radiocarbon dated to 11,159 years BP. In 1887 another almost complete and well-preserved specimen of the Giant Deer was found in a marl pit at Close y Garey, between Peel and St John's, and this can be seen today in the Manx Museum. Although many other remains of these animals have been found in the British Isles the Manx specimens are probably among the last known to exist in the world before the species became extinct.

PREHISTORY

It seems clear that the Isle of Man became separated from the land mass of Britain comparatively recently in geological terms - between about 12,500 and 11,500 BP. The latter date coincides with the ending of the Ice Age and the beginning of the 'Holocene' period, during which a rapid global warming raised temperatures by as much as 8 degrees centigrade in a period of between 100 and 500 years. So, quite suddenly, in the terms of the vast time frame with which we have been dealing, the Island emerged with a shape very similar to that of today and with a temperate climate little different from our own. It is likely that the sea levels were between three and five metres higher than they are today at some point in the Holocene, and this is dramatically illustrated by the raised cliff-line at Blue Point in the Ayres. The present Island, which is some 52.3 kms long by 21.7 kms at its widest point,

19

Cashtal Yn Ard (Miles Cowsill)

covers about 500 square kilometres and is mostly composed of low upland. It is dominated by two ranges of hills, the larger of which is in the north and includes Snaefell, the highest point, at 621m, with North Barrule second at 565m. The southern range is less dramatic, with its highest point at South Barrule, 483m, and the two ranges are separated by a central valley. At first grass and shrubland established itself on the Island, followed by juniper, birch and willow trees from about 11,000 to 10,250 BP, soon followed by hazel, oak and elm, so that except for the high ground the Island was mostly forest, with peat marshes on the northern plain.

People arrived on the Isle of Man about 9,000 years ago, presumably linked to those who moved north and west from Europe to colonize the British Isles as a whole. There is little trace of these earliest Island residents except for a large number of flint tools which have been discovered, often close to the sea. The period from 7,000 to 4,000 BC is known as the Mesolithic and the people alive then are thought to have been chiefly 'hunter-gatherers' taking or hunting their food from the land or the sea and being constantly on the move. Glen Wyllin can claim to be the place on the Island where human occupation has been first dated from a number of flint weapons or tools, and there are altogether more than 80 recognized early Mesolithic sites on the Island, mostly near the coast. This is a large number compared with other areas bordering the Irish Sea. There are many more sites from the later Mesolithic period and altogether 320 of them have produced heavy-bladed flint tools. These are different in design from the earlier finds and more typical of contemporary tools discovered in Northern Ireland, a fact which has led some archaeologists to speculate that the Island was abandoned for as long as a thousand years and then recolonized from the river Bann area of Ireland around 5,000 to 4,000 BC.

During the two thousand years of the Neolithic period (4,000 BC to 2,000 BC) there was a change from the nomadic, hunter-gatherer way of life and there is far more evidence for permanent settlements and farming of the land because of the discovery of stone axes, pottery, and monuments made of wood and stone. The first millennium of this period saw the construction of several 'megaliths' (monuments made of large stones) which are impressive even today despite more than five thousand years of decay. The Meayll (or Druid's or Mull) circle is to be found on a hill above Cregneish in the south of the Island and it looks today much the same as when it was first described in 1863. There are six roofless T-shaped burial chambers, for cremated bodies, built of slabs of stone and arranged in quite a large circle. It was excavated in 1893 by young Philip Kermode, later the first Director of the Manx Museum, and flints including two leaf-shaped arrowheads were found in the chambers as well as sherds of early Neolithic bowls, which are distinctive round-bottomed pottery. The whole site was probably once a large circular cairn and it commands splendid views of the south of the Island and the sea. Its circular plan with chambers radiating from the central axis is unique in the British Islands.

The most impressive of the Isle of Man's Neolithic monuments is Cashtal Yn Ard, which lies on a spectacular site below North Barrule. It was first recorded in the early 19th century as an almost rectangular cairn about 30.48 metres long, but many of the stones which had once made up the cairn were regrettably removed in the middle of the century and used for house building. The site was excavated in 1935 and it revealed that there had once been an impressive paved forecourt leading to a large burial chamber divided into five compartments. The substantial slabs of stone that still stand upright and the almost magical quality of the site, surrounded by majestic scenery, make this one of the most evocative places on the Island. Spend a few moments there quietly and the Neolithic peoples suddenly do not seem to be so very far away.

The two separate sites above Laxey known, quite unsuitably, as 'King Orry's Grave', have unfortunately been surrounded by houses and divided by a road. The western site has an unexcavated chamber but the

21

larger eastern structure was excavated in 1953 and 1954 and revealed a cairn base, kerb, forecourt and chamber, with sherds of a plain Neolithic bowl and traces of a burial. It is possible that the façade of the forecourt stood some 2.43 metres high. There are lesser Neolithic sites at Lonan ('The Cloven Stones'), Kew ('The Giant's Grave') and Ballaharra. It seems clear that the major sites were used for cremation rituals and burial and were a focal point for the locality, just as the parish churches became much later. They were constructed on sites which had been selected for their prominence and cleared of woodland. Also set in clearings and dating from this period are low mounds of freshly broken quartz, found at a number of different sites to the north of South Barrule and to a lesser extent on Slieu Dhoo.

During the war of 1939-45 the Admiralty spent a great deal of money and effort on the enlargement of Ronaldsway aerodrome and while it was under construction in 1943 the contractors stumbled across a spectacular find dating from the second millennium of the Neolithic period. This was an oblong dwelling house about 7.3 metres long by about 4 metres broad with a hearth near the centre. The roof was probably held up by wooden posts, fourteen of which have been traced. It would seem that the house was occupied by a sizeable family in settled conditions and that they kept cattle, sheep and pigs. Many stone tools were found, including polished axe heads and hammers together with flint tools such as saws, chisels and knives and a humped-back scraper which seems to be an Island feature. A good deal of crudely made pottery was found including round-bottomed jars varying in height from 15cms to as much as 40 cms, probably used for storing food. The house also contained five very thin, oval-shaped slate plaques about 7cms long decorated with geometrically shaped chevrons and lozenges. Nothing comparable to these has been found elsewhere in the British Isles though there are similarities with artefacts found in Spain, Portugal and Ireland, emphasizing the significance of the Island's location on the Atlantic coastal routes. The finds at Ronaldsway are so important and so distinctive that they have been dignified with the status of a 'Ronaldsway Culture'.

All the evidence suggests that the Neolithic gave way to what we call the 'Bronze Age' (c. 2000 to 500 BC) without significant upheaval. The main technological difference was the widespread use of copper instead of stone and flint to make weapons and implements, and the first copper axes can be dated from about 2,200 BC. Copper was first used in the Mediterranean and the new technology probably reached Man from Ireland where it became well established, along with the manufacture of gold items. The Bronze Age is generally subdivided into Early, Middle and Late to correspond with changes in the style and design of implements and pottery. In the Early period flat bronze axes were the norm and several of these have been found on the Island, some of them decorated in the Irish manner. One drinking cup has been found at Baroose as well as three examples of pottery food vessels, one a fine specimen from Cronk Aust. During the Middle and Late Bronze Age more elaborate bronze axes were made together with bronze swords and spearheads and examples of all of these have been found, generally in lowland coastal sites. There was a major copper source at Bradda Head and it is likely that this was used for the manufacture of bronze items.

By now most of the earlier woodland had been cut down to permit farming and there is evidence of family settlements at Ronaldsway and Billown. Burials tended now not to be in public sites but in individual graves, usually a 'cist', or stone box in the ground. Into this the body might be laid, or an urn containing its cremated remains. Then the grave was covered over with either a stone cairn or earthen barrow. Some 400 of these Bronze Age burial sites have so far been identified on the Island and it is probable that many more have been destroyed in the recent past. Sometimes there is a circle of standing stones or quartz boulders round the central cist, such as at the Orrisdale circle or the two stone circles at Arragon Mooar. There are also many solitary standing stones around the Island, but they have not been dated and it is not clear whether they belong to the Bronze Age or the Neolithic, or indeed what was their function.

There are fewer visible relics of the Later Bronze Age, and it has been suggested that from the seventh and sixth centuries BC the climate deteriorated significantly in Western Britain, Ireland and the Isle of Man where the weather became cold, wet and windy, leading to a reduction in the amount of Atlantic trading. On the summit of South Barrule there are some 70 circular stone structures and a few of these were excavated in the 1960s revealing a hearth and pottery which suggested a settlement dated at around 1,000 BC. About 400 'burnt mounds' have been uncovered, mostly in the north of the Island, consisting of a patch of charcoal a few metres wide containing freshly broken pebbles. It is possible that these may have been a method of heating water over hot stones.

Chapter Two
The 'Celtic' Island

WHAT DOES 'CELTIC' MEAN?

From about 700 BC onwards iron began to be used in the British Isles instead of copper, so archaeologists have called the period from then until about 500 AD 'The Iron Age'. It seems to have been a time when it was necessary to defend local communities because hill forts were built, some of them, like Maiden Castle in the south of England, very large and ambitious in design. On the Isle of Man there are four or five hill forts and about 20 promontory forts, though no iron weapons or implements have been found. The most impressive hill fort is at South Barrule and it consists of an inner earthwork, stone built outer defences and about 70 small round houses. Much of it has been dated to the Bronze Age, but it is likely that it remained in use well into the Iron Age.

During the 1939-45 war a distinguished German archaeologist, Dr Gerhard Bersu, was interned on the Island but he and his wife were given permission to carry out a number of archaeological projects. One of these was the excavation of three low mounds at Ballacagen and Ballanorris, north of Castletown, each about 30 metres wide. Many original timbers survived and Bersu came to the conclusion that he had uncovered huge round houses whose roofs had been held up by a forest of timbers and he suggested that these were the dwellings of a tribal chieftain and his entourage. This is the line taken by the fascinating reconstruction to be seen in the House of Manannan at Peel but it has been challenged by recent researchers who take the view that the site in fact represents a number of normal-sized round houses enclosed within a wooden stockade. Beyond doubt is the fact that the site gave ample evidence of the rearing of domestic animals such as oxen, sheep, pigs and horses and there were glass and bronze brooches and the remains of metalworking.

To what extent the inhabitants of the Island during the Iron Age ought properly to be described as 'Celtic' has become very controversial. As early as the sixth century BC Greek writers used the name 'Keltoi' ('strangers') to describe the tribes of tall, fierce warriors who expanded over the centuries to dominate Central Europe and strongly influence Spain, Italy, the Balkans, Greece and lands to the east. In 387 BC they were bold enough to attack Rome itself and raze it to the ground. However, their culture was non-literate, which is for historians a serious problem. They passed down their laws, traditions, poetry, myths and legends by word of mouth, so in most respects the details of their civilisation, including the languages they spoke, have been lost. By the first century BC these tribes were the dominant forces in France and it was Julius Caesar who eventually conquered them and brought them under Roman rule. He also noted that 'in their own language they are called Celts (Celtae), in our tongue, Gauls'.

During the Renaissance French scholars began to emphasize their links to the ancient Gauls and in 1582 the Scottish scholar George Buchanan suggested that the early peoples of Britain were also descended from the Gauls and that Scottish Gaelic was derived from a lost Gaulish language. This view was strengthened by the eminent Welsh linguistic scholar Edward Lluyd in a study of British languages published in 1707 in which he suggested that the Gaelic languages then spoken in the British Isles and Brittany all derived from an ancient source which he chose to describe as 'Celtic', even though he did not know, and we still do not know, what languages the early European Celts actually used. Subsequent scholars have divided the British languages into two branches called Goidelic or Q-Celtic (Irish, Manx and Scottish Gaelic) and Brythonic or P-Celtic (Welsh, Cornish and Breton). The Revd William Stukeley, (1687-1765) enthusiastically publicized his view that 'druids' were the highly influential priests of the Celtic world, and he linked them (erroneously) to the mysteries of Stonehenge and other ancient sites. So the concept of a British 'Celtic' culture began steadily to grow.

Excavations at Hallstatt in Austria between 1846 and 1899 and at La Tène in Switzerland from 1874 dramatically revealed a wealth of physical remains and artefacts from a distinctive early culture whose menfolk were brave and reckless fighters as well as skilled metalworkers and who could produce weapons and jewellery of great craftsmanship and beauty, featuring intricate, curvilinear designs. These discoveries were widely accepted as being clear evidence for the existence of a European Celtic culture and they led in Britain to the growth of 'Celtic Studies' in many seats of learning during the nineteenth and twentieth centuries. The accepted theory for many decades was that the British Isles were steadily colonized from about 700 BC onwards by tribes of Celtic peoples from Europe who established dominant Celtic patterns of society, culture and language throughout the Isles.

However, recent archaeological research has seriously challenged this concept of a 'Celtic Britain' for the crucial reason that little evidence has been found for any significant migrations into the British Isles during the first millennium BC. It is now thought more likely that the 'ancient Britons' and their languages and customs gradually evolved in varying forms and that it is misguided to think of them in terms of being a Celtic race with traditions and languages imported from tribes of Central Europe. In the early 21st century, at a time when the parliamentary assemblies of Scotland, Ireland, Wales, and indeed the Isle of Man, are at last beginning to enjoy flexing their constitutional muscles, this is potentially quite a blow to the concept of a 'Celtic' national identity.

The British Isles were known to be rich in tin and it was this that lured the Roman general Julius Caesar to them in 55 or 54 BC after he had defeated the tribes of Gaul. This expedition was only exploratory but in 43 AD the Roman Emperor Claudius ordered a full-scale invasion of Britain which was duly carried out, despite the spirited resistance of the native population. Wales was conquered by 78 AD but the Romans decided eventually that North Britain was unconquerable and the Emperor Hadrian ordered the construction of a massive wall extending from the Solway to the Tyne, which was completed about 122 AD.

The Romans made no serious attempt to conquer Ireland, which at that time was divided into about 80 petty kingdoms, most of them busily fighting each other. They also seem to have left the Isle of Man alone, except possibly for a degree of limited trading. Only five specifically Roman coins have been found on the Island, three of them in Castletown and one each in Santan and Onchan. If the Romans had incorporated the Island into the province of 'Britannia' we would know a very great deal more about life on the Island at this time and there might be roads, temples and villas to uncover. As it is, we know next to nothing in detail about the Isle of Man during the four hundred years or so of the Roman occupation of Britain. It seems likely that the Island's population of perhaps a few thousand lived peacefully in their round house settlements, farming and fishing and occasionally trading with visitors from Ireland, Britain and beyond. As Roman ships regularly carried provisions from Chester to the western end of Hadrian's Wall they must sometimes have passed within sight of the Island and it is possible that tribute-paying arrangements (or protection money) existed between the Islanders and the Romans.

Julius Caesar wrote in 54 BC that in the middle of the 'channel', by which he probably meant the Irish Sea, there was an island, which he called 'Mona'. The Latin word for mountain is 'mons' and it is possible that he used this word because the Isle of Man does indeed look like a mountain or mountains rising from the sea. However, this is also true of Anglesey, which the Romans also called 'Mona'. The Roman writer Pliny the Elder provided in 74 AD a list of the islands between Britain and Ireland and mentioned 'Mona', (probably Anglesey), and also 'Monapia', which might be the Isle of Man, while the geographer Claudius Ptolemy, writing in 125 AD, called it 'Monaoida'. So, as far as a historic search for the Island's name goes, it seems to have been called 'Mon' with varying additives by the Romans. In Irish it was called 'Manann', in Welsh 'Manaw', in the Icelandic Sagas 'Mon', and the earliest surviving inscription of the name on the Island is 'Maun', found on a cross in Kirk Michael.

The Island's people worshipped natural phenomena and believed in mystical powers and the arts of magic and in early literature and legend the Island appears as a distant, exotic, romantic location untouched by either military exploits or political ambition and far more remote from the contemporary world than it was in fact. The most important legendary figure associated with this Island of spirits was 'Manannan mac Lir', (the little one from Man, son of the sea) described much later by Cormack's tenth century glossary of difficult or obsolete Irish words as

> A wonderful trader who was from the Isle of Man. He was the best pilot who was in the west of the world. He would know through his sky-gazing, that is looking at the state of the heavens, that is the air, the length of time the fine weather would last, and see the bad weather, and when it would change from one to the other. The Gaels [and] the British called him the god of the sea, and they said he was the son of the sea. (Hence the Irish speakers and the British speakers called him the god of the sea and they said he was the son of the sea) that is mac lir. The Isle is called Man from the name Manannan (and it is from him that the Isle of Man is called).

27

The last line is open to dispute and it is more likely that the reverse was the case and that he was indeed 'the little one from Man'. However what really matters is that the mysterious Manannan has persisted throughout its history as the Isle of Man's mythical friend and protector, making it invisible with his 'Mannin's' cloak of mist at times of danger.

It is not possible to say exactly what language was spoken by the inhabitants of Man up to about 900 AD (when it is clear that many were speaking Norse), though it can be assumed to have been a variant of one or more of the Gaelic languages. The Knoc y Doonee stone, found at Andreas and dated at about 600, has inscriptions in two Gaelic languages, Brythonic and Goidelic, and in two scripts, Latin and Ogham. It is possible that the form of some Island place-names current today are pre-Scandinavian Gaelic survivals, such as Douglas, from the Gaelic 'Dubhglais', meaning 'dark water' and Rushen, from 'roisean' or 'small moor or heath'. 'Slieau' comes from the Gaelic for moor or mountain land', while 'keeill' is a small church, and 'carrick' a rock. Recent opinion places the use of the frequently found Gaelic name-form 'balla', meaning homestead or settlement, well after the Scandinavian period.

The ancient Britons are known to have regarded tribal or family land as being held in common and they divided it into thin strips which were distributed among individuals for agriculture, while cows were put to pasture on common land. In the Island the length and narrowness of land divisions subsequently called treens or ballas would seem to reflect this pattern. We know more about early society in Ireland than the Isle of Man, but it is likely that the two were very similar. People in Ireland would be organized around a tribal chief, or king, who would be assisted by a few high status individuals and a body of freemen above the unfree men, or slaves. The free man would probably own several one-roomed round houses made of wood and wicker-work in which his family and followers were accommodated. The main garment worn was a loose woollen shirt reaching below the knees of the men and to the feet of the women and being of different colours and patterns varying from spotted to chequered. Over this was worn a tunic and a shawl, fastened at the left shoulder by a brooch. The legs of the men were generally bare, which must have been a trial in the winter. The body was often tattooed with woad and a good many bangles and bracelets were worn by those who could afford them. Food probably consisted of oatcakes, curds, butter, fish, onions, watercress and meat from domestic animals, and the main drink was ale.

It was the chief's duty to protect the people of his tribe and free tribesmen had the right to bear arms, which might be a pike or lance, short sword or shield. There is little doubt that the large hill fort on South Barrule was still in use during this period and a number of promontory forts were built on the headlands near river-mouths, or on the banks of some rivers. There were also look-out points at various places in the Island, still commemorated today by place names such as 'Cronk ny Arrey', or 'Hill of the Watch'.

CHRISTIANITY AND THE EARLY MANX CROSSES

Although the Romans made practically no impact on the way of life in the Island, Christianity certainly did. According to the Christian calendar, Jesus Christ was crucified in Jerusalem about 33 AD and for many years after this his followers were persecuted by the Roman authorities, though in fact this resulted in a dramatic strengthening rather than a weakening of the movement. Christ's chief disciple, Peter, travelled to Rome and established himself as leader (bishop) of the Christians there. He was executed in Rome about 64 AD, but his successors, emphasizing that Christ had made Peter his chief disciple, eventually claimed for themselves authority over Christians everywhere. Christianity received a tremendous boost during the reign of the Emperor Constantine (312-337) because he not only tolerated Christian worship but is said to have become a Christian himself. In 325 a Church Council met under his influence at Nicaea and produced a 'creed', or statement of beliefs which were declared to be the official basis of Christianity, and still are. In 391 the Emperor Theodosius ordered that Christianity would be the official religion of the Roman Empire and that pagan temples would be closed.

Christian churches were dedicated throughout the Roman Empire, including Britain, but the Empire itself came under heavy attack from Germanic tribes and Rome was sacked in 410. After this the Romans abandoned Britain and recalled their legions for defence nearer home. Britain, though not the Isle of Man, was gradually settled from about 430 onwards by pagan 'Angles and Saxons' from Germany and 'Jutes' from Denmark. They worshipped the pagan god Wodin and under them the Christian churches more or less disappeared.

In response to this challenge a number of brave spirits made it their

Irneit's cross-slab, Maughold. (Manx National Heritage)

life's work to bring Christianity to Ireland, Scotland, Western Britain and the Isle of Man. Chief among them was Patrick (c.389–461) a Briton who was kidnapped as a teenager by Irish raiders and sold into slavery in Ireland though he escaped after a few years and trained as a priest. His main work was done in Ireland but he also made an impact in Scotland and the Isle of Man where his name was given to St Patrick's Isle, two parish churches (Kirk Patrick itself and Kirk Patrick in Jurby), seven 'keeills' and two upright stone pillars on which are inscribed early Christian crosses at St Patrick's Chair in Marown. Whether Patrick actually visited the Island is not known.

Ninian (died c.453) studied at a monastery in France before building an influential church called 'Candida Casa' at Whithorn in Galloway. He had a powerful local influence and it is possible that he was actually the first Christian missionary on the Isle of Man. Brigit (born c.453) had an enormous impact in Ireland and throughout the western half of Britain. In the Island she gave her name to Kirk Bride and several keeills. Columba was born in Donegal in 521 and was related to the ruling family in Ulster. He established a well-known monastery at Iona on the Isle of Mull in 563 which became the centre of missionary activity in the north-west, including Man. One of Columba's followers was called Molua and Malew is named after him, while Marown takes its name from Ronan, another follower. Other well-known Island places named after missionaries of this period include German and Braddan, Arbory (from Cairbre), Santan (from Sanctan) and Onchan (Conchenn).

The religious sites established at this time consisted of small chapels called 'keeills', about 170 of which have been discovered, though only about 35 are visible today and even those consist of just parts of the walls. Although they vary in size they are generally small and can hardly have been intended for communal worship on a large scale and indeed their precise function remains an unsolved problem. It is possible that they were used as family burial chapels and they are often surrounded by a burial ground. The precise date of the keills is very difficult to establish and none of the existing remains have been confidently dated to this Early Mediaeval period at which they were likely to have been founded. The most important keeill sites were on St Patrick's Isle and at Maughold where the discovery of several keeills within an earthwork indicates the presence of early 'monasteries'. The identity of the original 'saint' Maughold who gave his name to the foundation is uncertain, but there is little doubt that

Crux Guriat, Maughold. (Manx National Heritage)

Maughold was an active religious centre, and this is attested by the fact that some 20 of the Island's 65 or so early cross-slabs have been found within the confines of the present Maughold village and churchyard.

These monuments are marvellous survivals from the early Christian church on the Island. The oldest of the Island's inscribed memorial stones date from pre-Christian times and are marked with Ogham script in which letters are denoted by strokes cut into the stone. This was a script used in Ireland and five examples have been found in the Isle of Man. One of Philip Kermode's major achievements was to collect and number most of the Island's known crosses and place them for safe keeping either in the Manx Museum or in the churches of the parishes in which they were found and he described them fully in his book 'Manx Crosses', published in 1907. Under Christian influence a cross was drawn on a stone slab and the earliest examples come from Maughold. Stone number 46, dated c 650, is a cross-slab with simple geometric and hexagonal patterns etched on to it, while number 47, called 'Irneit's Cross-slab' and dated to the late 7th or the 8th century displays a clearly-cut hexafoil pattern, the 'Chi-ro' early Christian symbol and an inscription recording a Celtic bishop, Irneit. Also from Maughold is the magnificent 'Crux Guriat' (no 69), a monumental cross-slab of the early ninth century, about 213 cms high by 91 cms wide. The cross is indicated by hemispherical boss-heads and contains the inscription 'Crux Guriat', the Cross of Guriat, who is thought to have been an early chieftain, or king, in Man. Cross number 96 at Maughold is a large rectangular slab with a ring-headed cross in low relief. Dated to the ninth century it has carvings of two seated religious figures thought to be the Coptic saints Paul and Anthony.

Outside Maughold there is a splendid tenth century cross-slab with dog-headed figures (no 92) which is to be found in Onchan parish church. The 'dogs', with their gaping jaws, might be representations of a lion. At Braddan there is a wheel-headed cross-slab from the ninth or tenth century showing two crouching beasts with a human face inside their open mouths. This is probably a pagan theme later used to depict the jaws of Hell. At Lonan Old Church can be found one of the most impressive stones of all (no 73), partly because of its design and size, and partly because it is quite possible that it is still standing on its original site. Some 152 cms high by more than 91 cms across it is decorated with tight interlacing with knots and plaiting on the shaft.

33

One of the most important examples of early art on the Island is the slab of stone depicting the Crucifixion which was found on the Calf of Man in 1773 when the ruins of an ancient chapel were being demolished. It remained in the finder's family until eventually purchased by the National Art Collections Fund and presented to the Manx Museum. When originally created it was probably an altar-frontal or reredos less than 90 cms tall and carved on a panel of Manx slate. The fragment that survives shows most of the figure of Christ on the Cross with his head erect and eyes wide open and clothed in elaborate garments. On the left is a spear-bearer, and it is likely that on the other side there would have been the figure of a sponge-bearer with an angel above each arm of Christ. This depiction of the Crucifixion, so different from the later representation of a dead and almost naked Christ figure, was part of the artistic tradition of the early Christian Church in the Eastern Mediterranean which reached Ireland in time for a version of it to be included in the late seventh century manuscript known as the Lindisfarne Gospels. There is a later version on an early eighth century bronze plaque from Athlone in the Museum of Ireland and the Calf of Man version may be a copy of this design.

While the Irish missionaries were successfully bringing Christianity to the west of Britain Gregory I, the Bishop of Rome, in 597 sent Augustine, the prior of a Roman monastery, to convert the pagan kingdom of Kent. He established a church at Canterbury and was appointed Archbishop of the English in 601 with instructions to found two archdioceses in England, one in London and one in York, with twelve bishops attached to each. By the time he died in 604 he had only managed to set up dioceses at Canterbury, London and Rochester but his follower Paulinus succeeded in converting King Edwin of Northumbria in 627 and founding a diocese at York. Eventually the two English archbishoprics were based on Canterbury and York, though they were never equal in size as initially intended.

According to the church historian Bede, writing in 731, King Edwin of Northumbria assembled a fleet in the year 625 and sent it to take control of Anglesey and the Isle of Man, possibly to evict rebels who were sheltering there. Bede writes 'He even brought the islands of Anglesey and Man under his power...The former of these, which is to the south is larger in size and more fruitful, containing 960 hides...while the latter has more than 300'. A hide was an area of land considered large enough to support one household, probably just over

The Calf of Man Crucifixion. (Manx National Heritage)

100 acres. In 664 one of Edwin's successors, King Oswy, convened a historic synod of Christian bishops at Whitby to work out a solution to the problems caused by the fact that Christian churches under the direct influence of Rome calculated the date of Easter and other festivals differently from adherents of the churches established by Patrick, Columba and others. The Synod decreed that the Roman rather than the Irish tradition should be observed in England but the priests of Ireland, the Isle of Man, Wales and parts of Scotland clung to their own traditions for many centuries to come.

Although Edwin of Northumbria sent an expedition to the Isle of Man in 625 he does not seem to have made a serious attempt to establish control over it and this was also the case with his successors. The other neighbouring power which might have had designs on the Island was the north Welsh kingdom of Gwynedd but again no takeover was achieved though it is possible that the rulers of Gwynedd collected tribute from the Island in the 8th century. The main contact between the Island and Britain during the seventh and eighth centuries is likely to have been between the monasteries at Maughold and Whithorn and many of the crosses found at Maughold have similarities with slabs found at Whithorn, especially the raised boss design of Guriat's Cross. It is possible that the monks at Maughold had come from Galloway and Northumbria and that they employed itinerant stonemasons from those regions to carve the crosses. Whether there was a significant monastery on St Patrick's Isle as well as at Maughold at this time must be left an open question, though a cemetery with graves from the 7th and 8th centuries has been discovered there. Maughold probably had several subsidiary cells on the Island such as at Ballavarkish in Bride or the Calf of Man chapel where the Cruxifixion stone was found, but as has already been stated, dating the Island's keeills is a difficult problem.

Chapter Three
The Vikings

SCANDINAVIAN SETTLEMENT

The eruption in the late eighth century of fierce sea-faring warriors, called 'Vikings' from the Scandinavian word for wanderers, is one of the major puzzles of world history. Why did these brave and hardy fighters decide to leave the fjords and inlets of their homelands in Norway, Sweden and Denmark and set out to row and sail across dangerous seas in small, though eminently seaworthy craft? Even now, after much scholarly debate, there is no agreed answer. Clearly the invention and development of the swift yet sturdy Scandinavian longships was crucial, for without them the ambitious journeys made by the Vikings would have been impossible. Theories advanced for the mass emigrations include a population explosion in Norway at this time and also the excessive growth of the power and authority of the royal house. In Denmark it seems that the custom of a family or tribe holding land in common was giving way to the passing of estates to individuals, often eldest sons, which implies that many men would be landless. Moreover there was, to these pagan warriors, the attraction of becoming rich by robbing the Christian churches and monasteries which had been established in many other countries. Above all, perhaps, to young men with the heroic deeds of the Scandinavian sagas whispered in their ears from birth, there was the pulse-quickening call of comradeship and adventure.

The distances they travelled are startling and destinations reached included Kiev, the north coast of America, Constantinople, northern Europe and especially Iceland, Greenland, Ireland and Britain. Most of the Vikings who attacked Britain came from Denmark and the first recorded raid took place on the east coast in the year 789. According to the Annals of Ulster Vikings first appeared in the Irish Sea in 795, making a raid on Rathlin Island. In 798 they returned and raided somewhere described as 'Inis Patraic', but this is probably the St Patrick's Isle near Skerries in Ireland rather than the one in Peel. Although Viking trading posts were established at Dublin by 841 there is no evidence of settlement either on the northwest coast of

'Odin's Raven', a replica Viking ship on view in the House of Manannan, Peel.
(DOT&L)

England and Wales or in the Isle of Man before the end of the ninth century, but it is very likely that raids took place - without leaving much archaeological evidence. Chester was occupied by Scandinavians in 893 and one of the first place-names with the Viking 'by' ending to be established in the region was 'Derby', on the Lancashire coast.

The Vikings worshipped the warlike gods Thor and Odin and regarded the death of a warrior as an opportunity to celebrate his status and achievements and also to equip his earthly remains with everything necessary for a life of feasting and fighting to continue in Valhalla. In Scandinavia dead warriors were either buried or cremated and their weapons were laid alongside, together with sacrificial offerings of food and drink and even horses and slaves. Armour was never buried because the Vikings believed that, once dead, they could be killed any number of times without suffering further damage. For warriors of major importance an entire ship might be buried containing the dead man and his belongings. Women of high status and wealth were often buried with their jewellery.

In eastern England the Danes arrived in force in 865 and established control over much of the north-east and East Anglia, which became known as the 'Danelaw'. Despite this extensive settlement only about 25 pagan burial sites have been discovered in the Danelaw, either because the initial pagan settlers were not very numerous or because they soon converted to Christianity. On the Isle of Man there are over 40 known Viking burials, which is proportionately more than any other part of the British Isles except for Orkney. Dating is again problematical but it seems likely that the Island was settled by Vikings from the late eighth century onwards and that the beaches of the north-west coast were the most suitable for the landing of their longships. Three Viking burial mounds have been excavated, at Ballachrink, Ballateare and Cronk Moar in the north-west of the Island and they contained swords, shields, spearheads, brooches, horse trappings and a range of other items. Two ship burials have been excavated, one in the north at Knock y Doonee and one in the south at Balladoole. At Peel as many as ten Scandinavian burials were found in an early Christian cemetery which suggests that, as in England, many Vikings adopted the ways of the native Manx fairly quickly.

Further evidence of this is provided at the Braaid, a site which shows that an earlier round house and farm had been enlarged by the

building of a rectangular Norse-style house and a curved or 'boat-shaped' one. Also, excavation of many of the early promontory forts, in particular Cronk ny Merriu, has shown that a Norse house was built on the existing site. Sir David Wilson, a Manxman, a former Director of the British Museum and an international authority on the Viking period, announced at his Presidential address to the Isle of Man Natural History and Antiquarian Society in 1994 that 'what these sites show is that there was a continuity of economy from pre-Norse to the Norse period, and we may be pretty certain from the evidence provided by the sculptured stones that the two populations — incomer and native — subsisted together and intermarried happily'.

THE NORSE CROSSES

The Norse crosses are among the most spectacular works of art ever produced on the Isle of Man. The pagan Vikings did not mark their graves with stones, let alone Christian crosses, but when they became converted to Christianity, probably after the first generation of settlers had died out, they adopted the idea of the carved cross with enthusiasm and produced their own versions, decorated in Norse

Gaut's Cross, Michael. (Manx National Heritage)

styles and with inscriptions written in runic script. This consisted almost entirely of straight lines which were easier to carve in stone and they seem to be based on Roman letters. Some 48 crosses found in Man belong to the Scandinavian period and most of them have been found in the northern parishes.

Two fine cross slabs, one from Andreas and one from Kirk Michael, are actually signed by the sculptor, named Gaut. The Andreas cross records that 'Gaut made this, the son of Bjorn from Kolli, (possibly Ballacooley), and the Michael cross has a runic inscription which has been translated 'Mael brikti son of Athakan the smith raised this cross for his soul's sake. Gautr made this and all in Man'. The significant point here is that Mael brikti (later Melbrigdi and eventually Bridson) and Athakan are Celtic names, yet they are commemorated on a Norse cross. Gaut's boast that he had carved all the Norse crosses of his day may well have been true when he made it. Clearly he was the son of a Viking and it seems that he spent his early life near Muncaster in what is now western Cumbria, where crosses of similar pattern have been found, before moving to the Island about 930. The Michael cross is decorated in the ring-chain interlace pattern, the Viking style commonly found in England and occasionally in Ireland, and both crosses have been dated to about 950. Several more crosses in the Island are probably the work of Gaut and his style was certainly copied by other stonemasons.

One of these was Olaf Liotulfson whose cross from Ballaugh is carved in Gaut-style interlacing patterns but with refinements such as bands decorated by pellets. A runic inscription has been translated as 'Aleif Ljotolfsson erected this cross to the memory of Ulf his son'. Another cross from Andreas is decorated with a goat and a ram and a hound leaping onto a deer and the runic inscription translates 'Sandulf the black erected this cross to the memory of Arinbiorg his wife'. Joalf's cross-slab from Michael (No 132) has a long runic inscription which reads '[Joalf] son of Thorolf the Red erected this cross to the memory of Frida his mother'. Above the inscription there is a figure of a warrior, full-face with legs astride, holding a spear in one hand and a round shield in the other.

Four late 10th or early 11th century crosses from Andreas, Jurby, Malew and Maughold tell what appears to be the favourite story of the Island's Norse settlers, the legend of Sigurd. In the nineteenth century the composer Richard Wagner gave a new twist of immortality to this enduring tale, which is the basis of his great cycle of operas, 'The Ring of the Nibelungs'. Marshall Cubbon, a former Director of the Manx Museum, summarized the original Norse story in 1983 for his booklet on the Art of the Manx Crosses:

> Briefly the legend tells how Sigurd, destined to become a great hero of his people, is brought up in a king's household and instructed by the wily dwarf-smith, Regin, who tells him how Loki threw a stone and killed Otter, the great fisher. The gods had been made to cover the skin of Otter with gold to recompense his father, but the gold carried a curse for whoever possessed it, and Otter's father was slain by another of his sons, Fafni the serpent-dragon, who then took the gold.
>
> Sigurd persuaded Regin to forge him a wonderful sword from the fragments of his father's magic weapon, and being given the choice of a horse from the king's stables selected Grani, 'the grey one', on the advice of Odin himself. Thus prepared Sigurd set out with Regin to try and win Fafni's gold.
>
> Following Odin's advice Sigurd dug a pit and hid there (covered with branches) until Fafni the serpent passed overhead, when Sigurd drove his sword up into the monster and slew him. Regin called to Sigurd to cut out the serpent's heart, roast it and give it to him to eat. Sigurd in roasting the heart felt it to see if it were cooked, and so burned his fingers, which he then sucked. On tasting the dragon's blood he could understand the language of the birds, from whom he learned of the wily Regin's plans to kill him and steal the treasure on his horse Grani.
>
> After many later adventures the curse of the treasure had effect and Sigurd was finally slain for the gold by his foster-brother Gunnar. The curse still followed the treasure, however, and Gunnar was finally cast, bound, into a pit full of snakes, one of which bit him to the heart, and he died.

Many a Norse child had been rocked to sleep as one or more parts of this complicated legend were recounted and the Manx crosses depict various scenes from the story. Two from Malew show Sigurd roasting the dragon's heart and sucking his fingers (No 120) while number 122 shows Loki throwing a stone to kill Otter, the great

The 'Dragon Cross', Kirk Michael. (Manx National Heritage)

Thorwald's Cross Slab, Andreas. (Manx National Heritage)

fisher, who has a salmon in his mouth, and also Sigurd's horse Grani carrying the load of treasure on his back. A stone from Andreas (No 121) has on one side Sigurd roasting the dragon's heart and sucking his fingers, with his horse and the head of a bird behind him, with on the other side Gunnar being bitten to death when cast into the snake pit.

Other Norse stories are commemorated in cross-slabs, such as No 127 from Jurby which shows an armed, bearded figure thought to be Heimdall, Warder of the Gods. He is blowing his great Giallar-horn to summon the Gods to Ragnarok, the last great battle which, according to Norse mythology, would mark the end of the world. Thorwald's cross-slab from Andreas (No 128) portrays a scene from this battle in which Odin, with his raven on his shoulder and wielding his spear, is devoured by the Fenris wolf, which is later slain, along with all things in the world. On the other side of this stone a belted figure is shown bearing a book and a cross and trampling on a serpent, while beside him there is a fish, an early symbol of Christianity. The suggestion is that this side of the stone illustrates how the kingdom of Christ has now replaced that of Odin. The Thor Cross from Bride is richly carved with the figures of men, giants, birds, animals and dragons. On one side Thor is shown attacking a serpent or dragon and there are also scenes from the great battle between Thor and the giant Rungnir. On the other side there is a scene from Thor's fishing adventure with another giant, Hymni. In his famous book on the Manx Crosses Philip Kermode described this cross as 'the richest example anywhere known of such illustrations of the old Norse mythology'. Crosses of the Norse type were produced on the Island for about 200 years but by 1150, with the growth in influence of Rushen Abbey and the Latin culture of the Roman church, the runic inscriptions and Scandinavian imagery were considered old-fashioned and, indeed, pagan.

EARLY NORSE GOVERNMENT

Recent researchers are confident that from about 900 there was in the Isle of Man a central, royal authority and that the Island was either an independent kingdom or a sub-kingdom dependent upon one or another of the neighbouring powers - either the Anglo-Saxon kings of England or the Norse rulers of Norway, Dublin and Orkney. A century later the rulers of Man had successfully extended their authority to include the 'southern islands' ('Sodorenses' in Latin)

Cross no. 106, Ballaugh. (Manx National Heritage)

which included Islay, Mull, Skye and the Hebrides but not the 'northern islands' of the Shetlands and the Orkneys, and this growing maritime power was increasingly referred to as 'the kingdom of Man and the Isles'.

Unfortunately we know very little about the early Viking kings of Man. One of the texts of the Anglo-Saxon Chronicle describes how in 974 eight vassal kings rowed King Edgar of England on the river Dee as an act of homage. One of them is named as 'Maccus', who was 'king of many islands', and several authorities are prepared to see this 'Magnus' as being an early King of Man and the Isles, probably Magnus Haraldsson (c 962-976). True to their nature the Manx Vikings were interested in war and conquest and both Magnus and his brother Godred (c 976-989) involved themselves deeply in the political affairs of the Welsh kingdom of Gwynedd and attempted to win control over Anglesey. They in turn were put under pressure by the powerful and ambitious Earl Sigurd of Orkney who had the Isle of Man well within his sights.

It seems likely that the Island's rulers were able to undertake trade successfully because at least fifteen hoards of coins have been found, dating from between about 965 and 1070, as well as a large number of silver arm-rings - almost as many as have been found in the whole of Ireland - which were probably used as currency. Hoards of coins really indicate two main things - that at least some of the individuals in the community were prosperous and that the coins were buried for safety at a time of perceived political danger or instability. A spectacular hoard dating from the early 970s was discovered at Ballaquayle and consisted of more than four hundred coins as well as ingots, arm-rings, ornaments and silver. A hoard found in Michael in 1972 contained coins which were probably minted on the Island at a mint now thought to have been established about 1025. In 2003 another splendid hoard was discovered in Glenfaba, containing 464 silver coins, 25 ingots and a silver armlet.

Among the difficult problems to resolve concerning the Norse and pre - Norse periods on the Island are the origins and names of the present six sheadings and seventeen parishes and of the ancient treens and quarterlands and indeed of the two deemsters and Tynwald itself. There has been much discussion among experts and there are several possibilities but it is likely that the sheadings we know today are to some extent based on the tribal boundaries of the pre - Norse period and that each tribe may have had a central meeting place. The Vikings

St John's and Tynwald Hill. (Miles Cowsill)

built upon these foundations to create more effective administrative units with courts to deal with local disputes and the name 'sheading' is probably of Norse origin and may be linked to the requirement for each unit to provide war ships for the king.

The treens were units of land varying in size from about 200 to 400 acres and the name is thought to be Celtic in origin, though its meaning is not clear. It is possible that in Christian times a keeill was built in each treen. A treen was divided into four quarterlands, a name which may be connected with the Irish word for 'ounceland', a land unit used in the Hebrides and Orkneys by the Norse, and it is likely that during the Scandinavian period in Man each treen was required to provide four fully-equipped men to serve in the war galleys, one from each quarterland.

The origins of Tynwald stretch back into pre-Norse times when there was probably a central meeting place in each sheading and perhaps one for the whole Island. Certainly the Tynwald mound at St John's is far older than the Scandinavian era and might well go back to the Bronze Age. It seems that a pagan 'fair' was held here on Midsummer Day, during which business was transacted and games were played. In Christian times the place was named after the saint whose feast day was the closest to this day, St John the Baptist, (24 June), and its Celtic name is still 'Cronk y Keeillown', the hill of St John's keeill. The Vikings brought with them their practice of holding a yearly open-air assembly of all freemen at which new laws were announced and where arguments could be settled and business transacted. This assembly was called 'Thing' by the Norse and their name for a meeting place was 'Vollr' - hence 'Thingvollr' and later 'Tynwald'. In 1979 the Isle of Man decided with much fanfare to celebrate the 'Millennium of Tynwald', which would have placed its origin in 979 when either Magnus (the rower) was king or his brother Godred. While a 'Thingvollr' might well have been held in that year (or even earlier), it has to be said that there is no evidence for it.

Well before the arrival of the Vikings it seems that the Island was divided into the 'Northside' and the 'Southside', with the three sheadings of Glenfaba, Michael and Ayre in the north and Garff, Middle and Rushen in the south. The division was emphasized by the geographical features of the Island, which made it difficult to cross from one side to the other, and this led to the development of different customs and also dialects and to some aspects of Manx life that are still apparent today. A surviving feature of these ancient divisions are the two deemsters. Originally there was one law-giver for each of the two 'sides', and his Gaelic name was 'Briw', while the Norse called him 'Lagman'. In the 15th century the English term 'Deemster' came into use and there remained a Norther Deemster and Southern Deemster until 1918 when the titles were changed to First and Second Deemster, though for legal purposes the sheadings in each side were altered in 1796 with Michael, Ayre and Garff in the north and the rest in the south.

Between about 900 and 1000, therefore, the internal organization and the administration of the Isle of Man developed steadily under its Viking kings. They were also very successful during this century in spreading their influence far to the north of Man to include many islands, chief of which were Islay, Mull, Skye and Lewis, the 'Sodorenses' or southern islands, though they did not establish control over the Orkneys and Shetlands. By 1000 this maritime 'Kingdom of Man and the Isles' had emerged as one of the significant powers jostling for control over the Irish Sea area. Its rivals included various Irish chieftains who established themselves as kings in Dublin, Leinster and Munster, and also the Earls of Orkney, though the most formidable adversaries were the kings of Scotland and Norway. The story of Manx history over the next 250 years would be that of a scattered island kingdom struggling to survive and develop in a sea of predators, where the guiding principle was very much that of the survival of the fittest and the strongest.

Chapter Four
The Kingdom of Man and the Isles, 1079-1156

THE CHRONICLES OF THE KINGS OF MAN AND THE ISLES

The rulers of the extended kingdom of Man and the Isles in the early eleventh century came from one of three Irish royal families. These were the descendants of Harald of Limerick (to 1005), Sitric 'Silkbeard's' family from Dublin (intermittently from 1005), and the Mac Ragnaill dynasty from Waterford (intermittently from 1046-1075). It seems that a member of this family, Echmarcach, having been overthrown as King of Dublin, was Man's ruler from 1052 onwards, though in 1061 the Island was invaded by the new ruler of Dublin who defeated him in battle and exacted tribute from him as a client king. So these kings of Man must be seen as being closely linked to their Scandinavian compatriots who held sway over several of the petty kingdoms of Ireland. Indeed the Irish connection is emphasized by one of the earliest surviving buildings on the Island, the round tower on St Patrick's Isle, which was probably an addition to an existing stone church. It is similar in design to towers in Ireland and both the church and the tower are thought to have been built between 950 and 1050.

The first definite names of Manx kings provided by written evidence are Godred, son of Sitric, who is recorded as being King of Man in 1066 (presumably the successor of Echmarcach, who died in 1064) and as having died in 1070, to be succeeded by his son, Fingal. This information is provided in a single copy of 'The Chronicles of the Kings of Man and the Isles', which is the only surviving Manx record of this period. It describes events in the Island from 1016 to 1377, chiefly the political and military activities of the rulers and the affairs of the bishops and the Church. Much of early Manx history would be literally lost without it but it presents considerable problems because its information, especially regarding dates, is often unreliable. It is likely that the 'Chronicles' were written by several monks of Rushen Abbey between about 1257 and 1377. The abbey was dissolved in 1540 and in 1620 the manuscript, written on about

51

23 parchment folios measuring 15cms by 13cms, found its way into the collection of the famous antiquary Sir Robert Cotton, where he had it bound together with a number of other documents, mostly unrelated to the Isle of Man but of the same size. It survived a fire in the Cotton library in 1731 (somewhat scorched) and was transferred to the British Museum which bought the Cotton library in 1753, and to the British Library after 1972, where it remains as BL Cotton Julius A vii. For the sake of brevity this invaluable primary source will be referred to as the Chronicle.

GODRED CROVAN 1079-1095

Godred Crovan was closely related to the family of Sitric Silkbeard, King of Dublin, and his nickname 'Crovan' means, in translation, 'Godred of the Fingers', suggesting he had some deformity of one or both hands. His great-grandfather was Eric Bloodaxe, King of Norway, and it is possible that his father, Harald the Black of Islay, had once ruled in Man, which would explain why the Chronicle says that he spared the Manx in 1079 'since he had been reared among them for some time'. Godred's royal connections were cemented by his marriage to Ragnhild, a daughter of King Harold Hardrada of Norway.

In January 1066 King Edward of England died childless and the great prize of the English throne lay for the taking. It was coveted by three powerful men, none of whom had a legitimate claim to it, Earl Harold of England, the dead king's son-in-law; King Harold Hardrada of Norway, who aimed to win it by conquest, and Edward's cousin, William, Duke of Normandy who claimed that Earl Harold had sworn on oath to recognize him as king. In fact Earl Harold, who had the great advantage of being on the scene, lost no time in having himself proclaimed king and crowned by the Archbishop of York. He then prepared himself for two onslaughts, Scandinavian and Norman, which he knew were inevitable. The first came from Harold Hardrada who assembled a great fleet and army and landed on the north-east coast in September, sweeping aside the forces that initially confronted him. On September 25th he met King Harold at Stamford Bridge, on the river Derwent, and the English won what ought to have been one of the most decisive victories of the century. Hardrada, together with most of his army, was slain, and those who escaped from the field that day counted themselves lucky. It was Harold's great misfortune that only three days later William of Normandy was able to land

ꝯmū ĩ danmarc moꝛabꝯ· Anno ꝯ· xcii· ꝯ harald rex
ꝯundonꝯ · ⁊ ꝯ ꝯunꝑer ſepelit· cui harðecnuꝯ ſuccesſit

Anno· ꝯ· xx·vii· ꝯ magñ rex noꝛwegie ſ̄cī olaui regiſ filiꝯ
ſᵤbacto rege danoꝛ ſuano danmarc ſibi ſᵤbiugauit·
anno ꝯ· xx·viii· magñ rex cū ſuano ꝑlimū cōmitcenſ
illū de danmarc expulit· ⁊ ĩ illa regnauit· ac ñ multo ꝑ
Anno ꝯ· xxix· ſuanꝯ dannichiā ꝛtiū recepiteꝯ obiit·
⁊ harald harphagre regiſ byⱳarði filiꝯ noꝛwegiam
recepit· Ipſe ū ex parte matꝛ frat̄ ſ̄cī olaui· pa꭛ruuſ
ſcilic; magni regiſ· hic cū angloꝛ rege ꝑ nuntioſ ſuoſ
pacem fecit· Eodem anno tꝛemoꝛ magñ extitit·

Anno ꝯ· xxx· ꝯ· Dux noꝛhymbruoꝛ ſⱳardꝰ iuſſu re
giſ eduuini ſcotiam cū multo exercitu intranſ ꝑlurſ
cū rege ſcotie coactheath cōmiſit illucq; fugauit· et
malcolmū ut rex iuſſerat regem conſtituit·
anno ꝯ· xxx·vi·   ꝯ· xxx·vii· ꝯ· xxx·viii· ꝯ· xxxix· ꝯ· xl·
ꝯ· xl·i· ꝯ· xlii· ꝯ· xl·iii· ꝯ· xl·iiii· nichƚ memoꝛie
Anno· ꝯ· xl· ꝯ· Noꝛnaloꝛ rex griffin a ſuiſ interficiꝰ
capudeq; cum oꝛnatura cōmiti haraldo mittiꝯ· ꝗð
mox ille regi edⱳardo detulit· rex ū edⱳardꝰ ꭓꭇā iꝑe
duobꝯ fꝛibꝯ ſuiſ conceſſit·   Anno ꝯ· xl· vi·
Anno· ꝯ· xl· vii· obiit pie memoꝛie edⱳardꝰ rex anglie·
de quo dꝝ ꝗð erat honoꝛ ⁊ gƚa angloꝛ dū uixit· ⁊ eoꝛdē
ruina dū moꝛit·

unopposed on the south coast and that he was forced to march his tired troops rapidly down south to meet Willam and suffer defeat and death on Senlac Hill (Hastings) on October 14th.

One of those who counted themselves lucky at Stamford Bridge was Godred Crovan. He was able to escape from the field and as his cousin was King of Man at the time he decided to take refuge there, where he was honourably received. He then disappears from view until about 1079 when, the kingship of Man presumably being vacant, he made three vigorous bids to be its ruler using warriors whom he had recruited in the Western Isles. According to the Chronicle:

> Godred Crovan mustered a great number of ships and came to Man; he joined battle with the people of the land, but was defeated and put to flight. Again he assembled an army and ships, came to Man, fought with the Manxmen, was defeated and put to flight. A third time he gathered a massive force and came by night to the harbour which is called Ramsey, and three hundred men he hid in a wood which was on the sloping brow of the mountain called Sky Hill. At dawn the Manxmen formed up in battle order and after a massive charge joined battle with Godred. When the battle was raging vehemently, the three hundred men rose from their place of hiding at their rear and began to weaken the resistance of the Manxmen and compelled them to flee. Now when they saw themselves defeated without any place for them to escape to, for the tide had filled the riverbed at Ramsey and the enemy were pressing constantly from the other side, those who then were left begged Godred with pitiful cries to spare their lives. Moved with compassion and taking pity on their plight, since he had been reared among them for some time, he called off his army and forbade them to pursue them further.
>
> The following day Godred gave his army the option of either dividing Man among themselves and living in it, if they so preferred, or of plundering the land entirely and returning home. It pleased them more to lay waste the whole island and to enrich themselves with its valuables, and thus to return to their homes. Godred on the other hand granted the southern part of the island to the few

islanders who had stayed with him, and the northern part to the remainder of the Manxmen, on condition that none of them should at any time dare lay claim to any part of the land for himself by right of inheritance. Whence it has come to pass that up until the present day the entire island is the property of the king alone, and that all its dues belong to him.

After the majority of his forces had taken their booty and returned to their homes in the Western Isles, Godred was left to rebuild the Island and to establish himself firmly in control of it. Eight years after Sky Hill Godred faced a determined attack from the rulers of Dublin, keen yet again to establish their overlordship of the Island. Godred not only defeated this expedition but slew its leaders and then successfully established himself as King of Dublin in 1091. Backed by a fleet of 90 ships he beat off an attack by the King of Leinster in 1094 but after Godred's allies had returned home the King of Leinster made a surprise return and he was forced to abandon Dublin. He died in the following year of plague, according to Irish sources, and on the island of Islay according to the Chronicle.

Godred was certainly a powerful force. Born of an Irish Viking royal house he had fought for the King of Norway in his attempt to conquer England, taken part in one of the great battles of the age and been lucky to escape with his life. He then used determination and guile to win for himself the kingship of Man and established strong control over it. This done, he won and lost the throne of Dublin and might have recovered it again but for his death from disease. It is quite clear that the kingdom of Man and the Isles had been in existence long before Godred's lifetime, but thanks to the Chronicle and its detailed account of the battle of Sky Hill we know far more about him than any of the earlier kings, many of whom might also have been warriors of renown. All the subsequent kings of Man down to 1265 were directly descended from Godred and this must surely give him a pre-eminent place in Manx history as a formidable warrior and leader and as the undoubted founder of a royal dynasty in the Island. The Manx version of his name Godred is 'Gorree' and up to the present day he alone of all the kings of Man has remained an immovable fixture in the Island's consciousness as the traditional 'King Gorree' or 'King Orry' of legend.

MAGNUS BARELEGS, 1098-1103

According to the Chronicle the events that occurred after Godred's death were as follows:

> He left three sons, i.e. Lagman, Harald and Olaf. Lagman, the eldest, seized the kingdom and ruled for seven years. However, Harald his brother rebelled against him for a good while. But at last he was captured by Lagman and deprived of his genitalia and eyes. After this Lagman regretted blinding his brother and abdicated the kingdom of his own accord. Marked with the sign of the Lord's cross he undertook a pilgrimage to Jerusalem but died on the way.....all the noblemen of the Isles, when they heard of Lagman's death, sent an embassy to Muircheartach O'Brien, King of Ireland, requesting that he send some active man of royal stock to act as regent until Olaf, son of Godred, became of age. The king very willingly assented to them and sent a certain Donald son of Tadhg to them, advising and instructing them to govern the kingdom with all due kindness and moderation, as it was not his. But after he arrived in the kingdom he thought little of his lord's instructions and abused the kingdom with great tyranny; he perpetrated many crimes and ruled ruthlessly for three years. Then all the chieftains of the Isles with one accord banded together in a body against him and drove him from their borders. He fled to Ireland and returned to them no more.

This is all good mediaeval history stuff, featuring rebellion, grisly mutilation, crusading and tyranny. However the Chronicle's account does not fit with information from Irish and other sources. Recent researchers consider it doubtful that Lagman was ever king in Man, though he might have ruled over one of the other islands, and even though he might well have castrated his brother it was not before Harald had sired three sons who later played a part in Manx affairs. Moreover it is possible that the Manx actually requested a regent from Muirchertach on the death of Godred Crovan in 1095 and that he sent his nephew Donald who unfortunately ruled in a such a ruthless way that he was driven out in 1098. After his departure civil war seems to have plagued the Island because the Chronicle says that 'there was a battle fought between the Manxmen at Santwat, and the men of the north obtained the victory. Earl Ottar and Macmaras, leaders of the two sides, were cut down in the engagement'.

At this point the youthful King of Norway, Magnus Barelegs, the grandson of Harold Hardrada, who later earned his nickname by wearing Gaelic dress and going barelegged while in the west, intervened personally to restore order in Man and also impose himself as overlord of the Island. He succeeded his father as King of Norway in 1093, aged about 20, and spent his first few years establishing his authority over rivals to the throne. This done, he looked to increase his influence further afield and the upheaval in Man gave him a good opportunity. He first sailed to the Orkneys and the Hebrides, bringing fire and the sword to Lewis, Uist, Skye, Tiree and Mull before beaching his ships on the Isle of Man. Clearly he liked what he saw, because according to the Chronicle

> When he landed at St Patrick's Isle he came to view the site of the battle which the Manxmen had fought a short while before between themselves, because many bodies of the slain were still unburied. Seeing the great beauty of the island, it was pleasing in his sight and he chose to live in it. He constructed fortresses there which to this day bear his name.

No Island fortresses bear Magnus' name in the 21st century, but archaeologists have discovered defences on St Patrick's Isle that can be dated to Magnus' period as well as a timber-framed building which might have been suitable as a royal apartment.

Magnus made some attempt to restore damage in the Island and called upon the men of Galloway to send timber. On an expedition with six ships he encountered the Anglo-Norman earls of Chester and Shrewsbury off Anglesey and he slew Hugh of Shrewsbury, bringing him no little repute among chroniclers of the times. He also appears to have made a treaty with the King of Scotland, who agreed that the western Isles should belong to Norway – though this was disputed by subsequent Scottish kings. Magnus then returned home where domestic affairs and a dispute with Sweden kept him busy for several years.

He set sail again in 1102, probably with the intention of establishing control over part of Ireland. He used Man as his base and decided to ally with Muircheartach, the King of Munster and Dublin, arranging a marriage between his son Sigurd, aged twelve, and the Irish king's daughter, who was five. The two men possibly had visions of using their alliance to assist a rebellion against Henry I in England as well as attacking other rulers in Ireland. However, Muircheartach was defeated by another Irish chieftain in August 1103 and shortly afterwards Magnus died in a fight in north-eastern Ireland, aged 30, and he was buried at Downpatrick. He had done rather more between the ages of twenty and thirty than the average young man and his feats were commemorated in two long-lasting Gaelic ballads.

OLAF I, 1113-1153, AND THE FOUNDATION OF RUSHEN ABBEY, 1134

Magnus' son Sigurd returned to Norway which he ruled jointly with his two younger brothers, who both died before him. He seems to have made no immediate attempt to claim the Isle of Man and there is confusion about events on the Island after Magnus' death. The Chronicle says that 'the chieftains of the Isles sent for Olaf, son of Godred Crovan .... who was at that time living at the court of Henry, King of England and son of William, and they conducted him home. In the year 1102 [1103?] Olaf, son of Godred Crovan, began ruling over all the Isles, and he ruled for 40 years'. Later on, when giving details of Olaf's disgraceful death, the Chronicle dates it at either 1152 or 1153, which would mean that he reigned for about 50 years, not 40. Some historians consider that Godred Crovan's eldest son Lagman re-appeared in 1103 and ruled until 1108, with Donald Mac Teige (the former tyrant) following him from 1108 to about 1113 when Olaf began his reign.

However, we can be sure that Olaf was indeed the youngest son of Godred Crovan and he had spent some years at the court of Henry I of England, son of William 'the Conqueror', who succeeded his brother William II (Rufus) in 1100 after his controversial death from a stray arrow in the New Forest. A.W.Moore states that Olaf's nickname was 'Kleining', or 'the Dwarf' but gives no authority for this and there is no mention of the nickname among the authors of the Island's most recent mediaeval history. Living at the centre of Anglo-Norman life would perhaps have made Olaf more cultivated and politically aware as well as bringing Man and the Isles well within the focus of Henry I, one of the ablest of English kings both as a warrior and as an administrator and lawmaker. Perhaps as a result of this education and upbringing Olaf ruled not only for a very long time, but also peacefully and diplomatically. The Chronicle says that he 'had all the kings of Ireland and Scotland as confederates in such a way that no one dared disturb the kingdom of the Isles during his lifetime'. He married Affrica, a daughter of Fergus of Galloway by whom he had a son, Godred. The Chronicle lamented that Olaf 'over-indulged in the domestic vice of kings', meaning that he had many concubines and illegitimate children, including three sons and several daughters. However, it was not too critical of him, being mindful of the fact that Rushen Abbey, the home of the monks who wrote the Chronicle, had been founded by Olaf. They therefore added that he 'granted lands and privileges to the churches of the Isles; and he was devout and enthusiastic in matters of religion and was welcome both to God and men...'

During his early years at the English court Olaf would have been familiar with Edward the Confessor's impressive abbey at Westminster which had recently been completed, as well as William Rufus' great hall, and it may well be that this experience led to Olaf's decision to establish an abbey on the Isle of Man. It seems that in 1134 he was prepared to give land in Rushen to the Cistercian abbey at Rievaulx in Yorkshire for the foundation of a daughter-house there, but the offer was refused. He then approached Ivo, Abbot of the Savignac abbey at Furness, with a similar offer, which was accepted. The Savignacs began at Savigny in northern France and were the favourite order of England's King Stephen, who granted them land near Preston in 1124. Three years later they relocated to a quiet valley near Furness and began to build a large abbey there and to establish daughter-houses wherever possible. Within twenty years they had founded 17 houses in England and Wales, two in Ireland, and the one at Rushen. In 1147 the Abbot of Savigny ordered a merger with the larger and more powerful order of Cistercian monks, a move which was resisted for a time by Peter, Abbot of Furness. He resigned in 1150 and Furness then became a member of the international Cistercian community of 'White Monks'. They had been founded in 1098 by an austere group of monks who were dissatisfied with the old-established Benedictine order which had, they considered, become lazy, worldly and decadent. The Cistercians lived very simply, attended scrupulously to their devotions, worked on their land and sited their monasteries in remote locations.

The first monks from Furness probably arrived at Rushen about

1138 but none of the surviving architecture can be dated from this period. Moreover, it seems that in 1192 the monks moved to Douglas for four years before returning to Rushen and they may well not have chosen exactly the same place. However, between about 1192 and 1230 the abbey was firmly established as a major religious and secular power on the Island, working a demesne farm of more than 1,000 acres which contained some of the most fertile land on the Island. The abbey had the right to appoint the priests at Lonan, Santan, Arbory, Rushen and Malew, enjoying a proportion of their tithes, and it served as a mortuary chapel for the kings of Man, though it is not clear whether they were crowned there. The main mystery about Rushen Abbey is why it was so small. Even in its heyday it was not big enough to house more than about 20 monks and the very modestly-sized church was one of the few in Cistercian houses in the British Isles to be without aisles. The cloister area is only about ten metres square, much smaller than in other monasteries. Still, Rushen did manage to survive and flourish, which cannot be said for the monastery at Myroscough in the north of the Island, which was founded in 1176 by Cistercian monks from Rievaulx Abbey in Yorkshire but languished in the next century when its lands were transferred to Rushen about 1250. In addition to the abbey at Rushen a small priory for nuns was founded in Douglas between 1187 and 1228. It was granted the right to appoint the priest at St Conchan's church (Onchan) and survived until 1540.

King Olaf can be credited not only with the successful establishment of Rushen Abbey but with a long and peaceful reign during which it seems there was only one, unsuccessful, attack on the Island, by the Welsh prince Cadwaller in 1142. During his reign Olaf was able to rule Man and the southern Isles with little interference from his theoretical overlord the King of Norway and there is some indication that the kingdom achieved an importance and credibility during his reign that it had lacked in earlier times. However, he came to an undeservedly ignominious end. In 1152, aware of the possibility of an attack on Man from King David of Scotland, Olaf decided to seek the protection of King Inge of Norway and sent his son Godred to do homage to him. While he was there Olaf's nephews, the three sons of his brother Harald who had been blinded and castrated years earlier by their other brother Lagman, took advantage of Godred's absence to sail from Ireland with a considerable force of men and lay claim to the kingdom of their elderly uncle. According to the account given in the Chronicle they came to Man

> demanding that half the entire kingdom of the Isles be given to them by the king. Now when the king heard that, he replied in his wish to placate them that he would take advice on the matter. And when they had arranged the day and place where the council should be held, those most wicked men in the meantime were discussing among themselves the death of the king. On the appointed day both parties convened at the port called Ramsey; they sat in rows, the king with his men on one side, the conspirators with their men on the other. Reginald, the middle brother, who was to strike him, was standing apart talking with one of the chieftains of the land. When he was summoned he came to the king, and turning towards him as though to salute him he raised his gleaming axe into the air and with one blow cut off the king's head.

GODRED II, 1153-1187 AND THE BISHOPRIC OF SODOR

After this shocking murder of their uncle the three brothers decided to capitalize on the situation and set sail for Galloway with the intention of seizing it as well. There, the Chronicle relates, 'the people of Galloway massed together and after a great charge joined battle with them. They straightway turned tail and fled amid great confusion back to Man. All the Galloway men living in Man they either slaughtered or expelled'. Meanwhile Olaf's son Godred made plans to rescue his inheritance and sailed back from Norway with five ships, stopping first at Orkney where he was received with enthusiasm and unanimously elected king by the chieftains of the Isles. He then sailed to Man where he secured his position by capturing his three cousins, putting one of them to death and blinding the other two.

While Godred had been in Norway doing homage to King Inge and possibly paying the ten marks in gold due to Norwegian kings on their accession, his visit is likely to have coincided with that of the papal emissary Nicholas Breakspeare (later as Adrian IV the only Englishman as yet to be elected Pope) who was there to set up the new archdiocese of Nidaros (Trondheim) as part of a widespread reorganization of the Christian Church. The bishopric of Man and the Isles was included in the new province and it seems likely that this

Rushen Abbey. (Miles Cowsill)

was the result of Godred's influence. There were probably bishops in Man in the pre - Norse and Norse periods but we have no record of them or of any diocesan organization because the Chronicle, in a section dealing with the bishopric, states that 'there have been many bishops in Man, but it is sufficient to begin the account of the bishops from Roolwer. We say it is sufficient because we are totally ignorant of what [or] which bishops there were before him because we have found no record, nor have we learned anything certain from the tradition of our elders'. Roolwer was bishop before the reign of Godred Crovan and he is buried at Maughold. He was followed by William, who was bishop during Godred Crovan's reign, and by Hamond, a Manxman by birth, from about 1090 to about 1125.

In 1134, the year that Furness agreed to establish Rushen Abbey, it was granted the right to elect a bishop for Man and the Isles and shortly after this the monks elected Wimund, who was consecrated by Thurstan, Archbishop of York. Wimund, though popular in the Isle of Man for his intellect, eloquence and jovial manners, made the serious error of involving himself in military affairs and attempted to take over land belonging to the King of Scotland, as a result of which he was captured in 1152, blinded, mutilated and imprisoned for the

St Patrick's Isle. The ancient tower can be seen above the late 14th century fortifications, which also surround the site of St German's cathedral. (Miles Cowsill)

rest of his life. He was succeeded in 1154 by Gamaliel, who was consecrated by the Archbishop of York, though in that year the Pope approved the transfer of the diocese to the newly-established archbishopric of Nidaros. His successor Reginald, a Norwegian, was said by the Chronicle to have been 'the first to receive the thirds of the churches in Man from their incumbents' and it is possible that this means that the bishop was beginning to make the Isle of Man his main base. Christian, from Argyll or Orkney, succeeded him, to be followed by Michael, another Manxman, 'a man of venerable life and famous for his good qualities, a monk in deed and habit'. He lived a long life and was buried in Fountains Abbey about 1203. His successor Nicholas was of royal birth - the son of Olaf I's sister - and he was buried at Bangor in 1217.

The existence of an increasingly effective Bishop of Sodor under the authority of a Norwegian archbishopric, in company with an influential Abbot of Rushen linked to an important Cistercian Abbey in England, brought greater stability and credibility to the kingdom and placed it securely within the international embrace of the Christian Church. This meant that even kings had to watch their step, because they could be subject to church punishments such as excommunication and interdict, and it was in Godred's reign that the Christian world was traumatised by the murder of Archbishop Becket in his cathedral at Canterbury in 1170, a spectacular example of the potential for conflict between church and state that existed across mediaeval Europe.

Chapter Five
The Kingdom reduced in size, 1156-1266

GODRED II AND SOMERLED

G odred's success in dealing with the rebels who had murdered his father evidently gave him a reputation for decisive leadership because the Chronicle says that

In the third year of his reign the people of Dublin sent for him to rule over them. Assembling a large fleet and a substantial army he came to Dublin and was received graciously by its citizens with much dancing. A few days after by common decision and agreement they elevated him into the kingship. When Muircheartach King of Ireland heard this he collected a countless host of Irishmen and hastened towards Dublin to expel Godred and to subject the place to his rule. When he came near to the town called Cortcelis he pitched camp and remained there. The following day he selected three thousand horsemen whom he put under the command of his half-brother called Osiblen, and sent him with aforementioned horsemen of the town to parley with the citizens, while at the same time also weighing up their capability. However, as they were approaching the town, Godred with his men and all the citizens of Dublin sallied forth amid great uproar and with great force rushed out against them, and began to weaken their resistance with such a thick shower of javelins that they immediately compelled them to turn tail. Osiblen, the king's brother, while attempting a brave resistance was surrounded by the enemy and perished with many others. The rest escaped because they had horses. When they returned to their lord they told him all that had happened. When the king heard that his brother had been killed, he mourned in sorrow, and in exceeding disquiet instructed his army to return home, each man to his own place. After a few days Godred returned to Man and let all the chieftains of the Isles return home.

This was a notable victory for a king of Man and the Isles over the ancient enemy and seemed to place Dublin securely under Godred's control. However, from this position of strength, over-confidence led him to make fatal mistakes. 'When he saw that he was firmly established on the throne', the Chronicle explains, 'and that no-one was able to oppose him, he began exercising tyranny against his chieftains, for some of them he deprived of their inherited lands, while others he deprived of their positions'. By this time in the medieval world there was a strong expectation, backed by the teachings of the Church, that a king should govern justly and that men had the right to resist an unjust ruler.

Thorfin, one of those dispossessed by Godred, decided to appeal to Somerled, the ruler of Argyll, for assistance in the unseating of the King of Man. Somerled was a Gaelic-Norse warrior with royal ancestry who married Ragnhild, a daughter of Olaf I of Man, and established himself as ruler of the Argyll region between about 1120 and 1140. Like many of his type he was ambitious and quick to seize an opportunity to extend his power. Somerled agreed that his son Dougal should become the new ruler of Man and Thorfin took him to many of the Isles, subduing the population and taking hostages. Godred set out by sea to meet this threat and Somerled also assembled a fleet of eighty ships. The two forces fought a major naval battle on the night of the feast of the Epiphany, January 5/6th 1156. Though there was 'much slaughter on both sides' the battle was clearly indecisive because on the following morning the two sides met and Godred agreed to divide his kingdom with Somerled.

The details of this division are not clear though Godred certainly kept the Isle of Man and probably retained some control over Lewis, Harris and Skye, while Somerled took over the islands nearest his base in Argyll, namely the Islay and Mull groups. In 1158 Somerled felt strong enough to challenge Godred for his entire kingship and attacked the Isle of Man with a fleet of fifty-three ships. This time the issue was decisive: Godred was defeated and forced to flee the Island and Somerled took over the whole kingdom. Godred travelled cap in hand to the kings of England and Scotland seeking assistance in recovering his kingdom but received little help. Then he sailed to Norway from where he was able to establish himself in the Hebrides until 1164 when Somerled was killed fighting in Scotland. With the help of the Norwegian king Godred then mounted an expedition to take him back to the Isle of Man where he successfully re-established his authority. Godred ruled in Man until his death twenty-three years later but his contest with Somerled had important consequences. These were that from 1164 until 1266 Somerled's descendants continued in possession of Islay and Mull and the kingship of Man and the Isles was significantly reduced in territory. Also the Isle of Man itself was further isolated from its northern possessions.

In 1171 a seismic change occurred in the world of Irish Sea politics because King Henry II of England, one of Europe's most powerful rulers who also controlled most of France, effectively conquered Ireland. As early as 1154 he had been granted the title 'Lord of Ireland' by the (English) Pope and in 1171 he crossed with 4,000 men to put this claim into effect. The lesser kings of Ireland were in no position to resist Anglo-Norman power and agreed to accept Henry's overlordship, and from this action subsequent English 'rule' in Ireland can be dated. In 1176 Godred formally married the mother of his son Olaf at a ceremony witnessed by the papal legate, Cardinal Vivian, and performed by the Abbot of Rievaulx, who was rewarded with land at Myroscough, in the north of the Island, for the foundation of a Cistercian house. Shortly afterwards Godred's daughter Affrica was married to the Anglo-Norman lord John de Courcy, who had helped Henry II conquer the eastern part of Ulster. This marriage brought Godred close to the main stream of Anglo-Norman affairs and culture and the de Courcys proved themselves to be generous patrons of monastic houses in the region. These included, perhaps, Rushen Abbey, the earliest buildings of which (c.1190) bear close resemblance to Grey Abbey in County Down, founded by Affrica. The Chronicle says that Godred died on November 10th, 1187, on St Patrick's Isle, which suggests that Magnus Barelegs' fortress and royal residence were used as such during this period. Godred had his moments of glory, such as his success in Dublin, but he lost his entire kingdom to Somerled for several years and managed to regain only half of it. Strangely, in the circumstances, it was in the lost half that he was buried, at Iona.

REGINALD I, 1187-1228

Godred left three sons but the only legitimate one was Olaf, whom his father had proclaimed to be his heir. He was only ten years old in 1187 and as the Chronicle put it the Manxmen thought that 'one who did not know how to look after himself on account of the tenderness of his age would be quite unable to govern a people subject to him'.

So they sent for Godred's eldest, illegitimate son Reginald, then living in one of the Isles, and he was proclaimed king. Reginald was highly respected as a warrior king who according to one saga 'was then the greatest viking in the western lands. It was three winters that he had lain out in his warships without coming under a smoky rafter.' His kingdom's substantial fleet was arguably Reginald's greatest asset, and a recent researcher has described the Manx king in this period as a provider of fleets for hire – either for cash or for political or territorial gain. Hence Reginald is found involving himself in military expeditions in Anglesey in 1193 and in Scotland at the turn of the century. In 1204 Reginald's brother-in-law John de Courcy was expelled from Ireland by his former allies and sought refuge and help from Reginald who provided 100 ships to assist de Courcy in a failed assault on Dundrum Castle on the coast of County Down. This interference in Irish affairs prompted a response from England's King John who announced that he was taking Reginald under his 'keeping, protection and defence' and granted him some lands in Lancashire - probably to keep the King of Man on side.

The King of France defeated English forces at the Battle of Bouvines in 1204 and John lost control of Normandy and most of his French possessions. His response was to make up for this loss with an increase in his authority over Ireland. In 1210 he mounted a major offensive there with 500 ships but was angry to find Reginald providing mercenary help to his enemies and punished him by sending an expedition to Man which spent two weeks ravaging the Island and taking hostages. Two years later Reginald formally did homage to John, receiving in return some land near Carlingford Lough, and he subsequently visited John's court in person. This was probably to enlist his support against the mounting threat from his half-brother Olaf.

It is a mark of the extent to which the kingdom had by now fallen under the influence of Anglo-Norman and Roman Christian, rather than Celtic or Norse, practice that Olaf was able to claim the throne on grounds of primogeniture and legitimacy. At the start of his reign Reginald had established the ten-year-old Olaf on the poor, uncultivated, rocky and mountainous island of Lewis, where he grew to manhood and exercised some degree of authority. About 1207 Olaf, by then aged around 30, appealed to Reginald to be given charge of one of the more prosperous islands but his reward for this presumption was to be captured by Reginald's men and taken to

Scotland where he was held prisoner for nearly seven years by Reginald's ally King William the Lion. When William died in 1214 Olaf was released and went on pilgrimage with a retinue of nobles to the shrine of Santiago de Compostella. On his return it seems he was prepared to live at peace with his brother who encouraged Olaf's marriage to his own wife's sister and again gave them control of the island of Lewis.

Meanwhile Reginald found himself in difficulties with some of the great powers. In 1217 he executed some Irish mariners who behaved aggressively on the Isle of Man and followed this up with an attack in Ireland itself. Henry III of England responded with demands that he should do homage and make amends for his excesses in Ireland and Reginald in turn sought the protection of Pope Honorius III, agreeing to pay homage and fealty to him and to hold the Isle of Man as a papal vassal and to pay 12 marks a year for the privilege. None of this went down well with the King of Norway, who resented in particular the homage paid by Reginald to the English king.

At this point Reginald's relations with Olaf took a turn for the worse because Olaf and his new wife were visited on the Isle of Lewis by Bishop Reginald of Sodor, who was making a tour of the churches of the Isles, and Olaf ordered a splendid banquet in his honour. The bishop refused to dine with him on the grounds that he had previously kept as a concubine the first cousin of his present wife, which was forbidden by canon law. So Olaf agreed to the annulment of his marriage and he instead married Christina, daughter of the Earl of Ross.

This was a disastrous move because Reginald's queen bitterly resented the repudiation of her sister and embarked upon a strategy which would have done credit to Shakespeare's Lady Macbeth. She sent a letter, appearing to be from Reginald, to their son Godred instructing him to capture and kill Olaf. Godred sailed to Lewis with this intention but Olaf just managed to escape and sought help from his father-in-law the Earl of Ross. His cause was supported by Paul, son of the Sheriff of Skye, and together with a band of followers they surprised Godred in 1223, killed all his men who did not take sanctuary in the local church and captured Godred himself, who was blinded and castrated. In 1224 Olaf landed with a fleet of thirty-two ships at Ronaldsway and forced Reginald to divide the kingdom with him. This done, he sailed north to his own islands.

Reginald (and his wife) were not prepared to leave it at that, however, and in 1225 he set out with an expedition to the Isles, supported by Alan, Lord of Galloway, though this came to nothing. Then Reginald levied 100 marks from the Manx on the pretext of visiting the court of the King of England, but instead sailed to Galloway and arranged a marriage between his daughter and Alan's son, Thomas. This was enough to alienate support for him in the Isle of Man, where, according to the Chronicle, 'when the Manxmen heard this they were extremely angry, and sending for Olaf, they made him their king'. This was in 1226 and Olaf held the fort for two years before Reginald, supported by Alan of Galloway and his brother Thomas, Earl of Athol, returned on the attack in 1228 and ravaged Man while Olaf was elsewhere in the Isles. The Chronicle laments the fact that 'they laid waste the entire southern part of the Isle of Man and plundered the churches, killed as many men as they were able to capture, and the southern part of Man was practically reduced to a desert'. But all was not lost because after Alan of Galloway had left for home, Olaf returned and recaptured the Island.

The final crisis of what had become a desperate civil war is recounted in some detail by the Chronicle:

> The same year in the middle of the night during the winter King Reginald came unexpectedly with five ships from Galloway, and the same night burnt up all the ships of his brother King Olaf, and of all the nobles of Man, at St Patrick's Isle. He then sailed round the land, and seeking peace from his brother he stayed at the port called Ronaldsway for about 40 days. Meanwhile, however, he cultivated all the islanders who were in the southern part of Man and drew them into association with him. Some of them swore that they would put their very lives at stake for him, until he obtained half of the Kingdom of the Isles. On the other hand King Olaf gathered all the people of the north of Man to support him, and influenced them to such an extent with his oratory, that their affections were firmly fixed on him. On the fourteenth day of the month of February, that is on the feast of St Valentine the Martyr, King Olaf came with his host to the place called Tynwald and there waited a short while. As Reginald his brother approached the place and arranged his host in battle array to meet his brother in combat, Olaf came forward with his

men to meet them, and making a sudden charge against them put them to flight like sheep. Then a band of wicked men came upon King Reginald and killed him on the spot, unbeknown however to his brother. But when he heard about it he was much moved; however, he never in his lifetime exacted vengeance for his death. Many fell in the conflict. There came freebooters to the southern part of Man and ravaged it and left it almost without an inhabitant. The monks of Rushen conveyed the body of King Reginald to St Mary's Abbey, Furness, and there he was buried in the place he had chosen for himself while he was alive.

The Chronicle portrays Olaf as a good and almost saintly figure, probably because he was the legitimate claimant to the throne according to canon law and also because Reginald treated him very badly. First of all he usurped his throne and banished him to Lewis for twenty years, then he made sure he was imprisoned in Scotland for a further seven years and then his wife sent her son to murder him. It is not surprising that Olaf had his supporters and despite his warlike reputation and credentials, Reginald failed signally to get the better of his brother either by military or by diplomatic means and finally he was killed by Olaf's men. Torn by fratricidal civil war the Isle of Man and its people were the chief losers during this turbulent period. No doubt the Chronicle's frequent references to the ravaging of the Island are to some extent conventional hyperbole but it is difficult to escape the conclusion that life for many of the inhabitants of Man at this time was likely to have been unpredictable and unrewarding, to say the least.

OLAF II, 1228-1237

Olaf, nicknamed 'Dubh', or 'The Black' - a reference to his hair - was not the only contemporary ruler in the Irish Sea region to have been locked in a desperate struggle with his relations because similar conflicts had for several years dominated affairs in Norway, Scotland and Orkney. Only Ireland was beginning to calm down to some extent under the overlordship of Henry III of England, who increasingly regarded the Isle of Man as being of strategic importance for his Irish operations. Olaf might have vanquished his brother but he was still surrounded by potential enemies, including Reginald's former ally Alan of Galloway and the descendants of Somerled who still controlled the middle islands, all abetted by the king of Scotland.

But the biggest threat was Norway which now emerged from a long series of civil wars, dating from the middle of the previous century, which had drastically weakened Norwegian influence abroad. Since 1217, however, the nation had united under the vigorous rule of Hakon IV who was determined to re-establish Norwegian authority everywhere, including overlordship in Man and the Isles.

Soon after Reginald's death it seems that Alan of Galloway seized Man in the absence of Olaf, who then sailed to Bergen to do homage to Hakon IV and ask for his help in recovering the Island. He also had to promote his own claims to the kingdom over those of Godred, the son of Reginald, who had once tried to murder him and had been 'blinded and castrated', according to the Chronicle. However, we must assume that Godred was able to overcome these disablilities because he too was at Hakon's court, pressing his claims to be his father's heir. Hakon clearly decided to 'divide and rule' because he sent a Norwegian expedition under the command of his own candidate, Uspak, whom he intended as ruler of the islands still under the control of Somerled's family. Taking both Olaf and Godred with him, Uspak attacked the Somerled faction at Rothesay but he was hit by a stone and killed. Olaf and Godred then sailed on to Man where they found yet another usurper in control, Torquil MacNeil. The Manx would not fight for him against Olaf, however, and Olaf and Godred agreed to divide the available Isles between them, with Olaf retaining Man. Not long after this Godred was killed attempting to exert his authority in Lewis, so Olaf was left in possession of the kingdom once more.

In 1235 Olaf travelled to England and attended the court of Henry III, who was anxious to secure him as an ally in the Irish Sea. In return for forty marks and substantial quantities of corn and wine Olaf paid homage and agreed to guard the English and Irish coasts in the interests of Henry III and to put 50 galleys at his disposal, if needed. Hakon IV was displeased with the news of this and summoned Olaf to Norway to explain himself. He set out but returned because of ill health and died, aged 60, on St Patrick's Isle on May 21st 1237 and was buried at Rushen Abbey. The years of his sole rule were scarcely less chaotic than the years when he had contested the authority of his elder brother and they emphasize the fact that the kingdom of the Isles had become increasingly fragmented and incoherent, subject to warring factions internally and the outside interference of more powerful neighbours.

HARALD I, 1237-1248

Olaf left several young sons, Harald, Godred, Reginald and Magnus. The eldest, Harald, a boy of fourteen, was recognized as his successor in Man without dispute and, clearly a spirited lad, he immediately set out for the Hebrides to confirm his authority there, leaving his kinsman Lochlann in charge of the Island. Harald was well received in Lewis and sent a deputation back to Man to represent him at a meeting of Tynwald in October. However, this meeting did not go smoothly because 'at the assembly itself, when for a long time they were hurling hostile words at one another and engaging in a bitter verbal contest, as no reconciliation seemed possible, the two factions leapt out of the meeting of the people and attacked each other with hostile intent'. Most of Harald's deputation were killed by Lochlann's men in yet another disgraceful episode. Harald bided his time but returned to Man the following spring, whereupon Lochlann fled by sea, taking with him his young foster son, who was Harald's younger brother. Despite Lochlann's treachery the monks who wrote the Chronicle had a soft spot for him because of his subsequent fate:

> The same day Lochlann fled from Harald with all his men and sailed to Wales. He took with him his foster son Godred, son of Olaf, a boy of good disposition. Then having sailed all that day and the better part of the night they were approaching the coasts of Wales. And when they were eager to enter their desired haven, suddenly an adverse wind blew up against them and a mighty storm arose and they were driven back from the port they were seeking and suffered shipwreck in some rocky place on those same coasts. Lachlann was practically the first man to get ashore, but when he heard his foster son Godred shouting from behind him, he jumped back into the ship, as he wished to sacrifice his own life for the boy. He took the boy in his arms and was doing his utmost to lead him down to dry land, but they fell from the upper to the lower decks of the ship and were both drowned together.

Yet Harald's troubles were far from over. He had refused to do homage to Hakon who in 1238 sent an expedition to Man led by his lieutenants Gospatrick and Gilchrist who dispossessed him of the Island and transferred its revenues to Norway. Harald withdrew to

73

the Isles and made several unsuccessful attempts to land on Man, after which in 1239 he decided to sail to Norway and make his peace with Hakon. He was still only sixteen and he spent two years at Hakon's court during which time he won the affection and respect of the king who in 1241 confirmed him as King of Man and the Isles. Harald arrived at St Patrick's Isle in 1242, was well received by the people, and settled down on Man to rule peacefully. He maintained good relations with Scotland and with Henry III of England, who made him a knight in 1246: but this aroused the suspicions of Hakon who summoned him to Norway and he travelled there from England and met Hakon in Oslo. That winter he courted Hakon's widowed daughter Cecilia and they were married in Bergen in 1248. Returning home by ship they encountered a storm off the Shetlands and the ship was wrecked and all aboard were drowned. The tragic loss of this promising 25-year-old ruler was a shattering blow, and we are told that 'his death caused grief to all who knew him'.

REGINALD II, 1249, AND MAGNUS 1252-1265

When the news of Harald's death eventually reached Man his brother Reginald II was proclaimed king in May 1249 but 24 days later 'he was killed by the knight Ivar and his men in a meadow near the church of the Holy Trinity in Rushen to the south of the same church'. Ivar may well have been in the pay of Reginald's cousin Harald, the son of Godred and grandson of Reginald I, who now seized the throne illegally, ignoring the claims of Olaf's youngest son Magnus. Hakon of Norway summoned Harald to his court to account for this offence and held him prisoner there. He then sent a Norwegian fleet bearing Magnus and his father-in-law John of Lorn to Man and they landed at Ronaldsway in 1250. However, John of Lorn began giving orders as if he were king of the Isles, which the Manxmen resented because they recognized Magnus as their king. When John failed to produce written authority from Hakon for his pretensions, the Manx did battle on St Michael's Isle near what is now Derbyhaven and John and Magnus were forced to withdraw. For about two years Man was probably ruled by Governors in the name of Hakon but in 1252 Magnus returned to the Island on his own, 'whereupon all the Manxmen received him gladly and made him their king'. He spent most of 1253 as an honoured guest at the Norwegian court and in 1254 he was confirmed by Hakon as King of the Isles and returned to Man. In 1256 Henry III of England conferred knighthood upon him, together with formal letters of protection. For the next few years it seems that Magnus, together with Mary his Queen, was a popular ruler who preserved peace within the kingdom and was a notable patron of the church.

In 1257 Magnus was present at the dedication by Bishop Richard of the church of St Mary at Rushen Abbey, but his chief act of generosity to the Church was his grant to it of St Patrick's Isle, thought to have been made in the same year. This had long been a major centre of Christian worship on the Island, with a church dating from pre - Norse times, and it had also increasingly become the residence of the Manx kings. The cathedral of St German was probably begun in the late 1150s after the appointment of the first Bishop Reginald, and it was built of rubble and sandstone in the shape of a cross with a short nave and eastern arm of the same width. A second stage of building probably began under the second Bishop Reginald (c.1217-1225) and was completed by his successor Bishop Simon (c.1225-1247), who was therefore not the founder of the cathedral, as claimed by the Chronicle. The original eastern arm was replaced by a longer one and the crossing was remodelled and new arches inserted. Bishop Simon established a chapter of secular canons to maintain the services, conducted according to the Use of Sarum.

Given that Magnus was a popular ruler who had the support of the kings of England and Norway, it might have been thought that his kingdom's future was assured, but this proved not to be the case. The main problem was the determination of the Scottish kings to bring the disjointed kingdom of the Isles under their control. As early as the 1240s Alexander II tried out the diplomatic option and sent delegates to Hakon to negotiate the handback of the islands won by Magnus Barelegs. These proposals were rejected and subsequent offers of a cash payment for the islands were refused. Alexander died in 1249 leaving a seven-year old heir but when this Alexander III emerged from his minority to take charge of Scotland in 1260 he continued his father's policy regarding the Isles and at first made diplomatic moves. When these failed a force under the Earl of Ross attacked Skye and Hakon responded in 1263 with a major expedition against Scotland, which was joined by Magnus in the Sound of Skye and which launched a successful attack on Kintyre. Hakon then put Magnus in charge of 60 ships which sailed up Loch Long and were carried overland to Loch Lomond. Meanwhile on September 30th Hakon's main fleet was lashed by an exceptional storm and some vessels were forced ashore at Largs where they were attacked by the Scots. The rest of the Norwegians landed the following day and beat the Scots back, putting out to sea again. So Largs was an indecisive conflict but it was soon followed by the death of the elderly Hakon in the Orkneys. Alexander made use of this opportunity to take control of most of the Isles, while Magnus retreated to Man.

It was clear that Alexander intended to send a full-scale expedition against Man so Magnus felt he had no alternative but to travel to Dumfries and pay homage to him. The Scottish chronicles described Magnus as a 'kinglet' ('regulus') ruling a petty kingdom ('regniculum'), but he was allowed to hold it from Alexander 'for ever', and in return he would provide hostages and ten war galleys when they were needed. For ever was not, on this occasion, a long time because Magnus died in November 1265 and the Chronicle says that he died at Rushen Castle and was buried in Rushen Abbey. This is the earliest reference to Castle Rushen, though it is thought that it had probably existed for thirty years, or even longer. Though he had been a not unworthy ruler, Magnus failed to leave an undisputed successor because his son, yet another Godred, was illegitimate. This enabled the predatory Alexander to claim possession of the Isle of Man which put the finishing touches to his campaign to recover the kingdom of the Isles. In July 1266 Alexander concluded the Treaty of Perth with the new King of Norway who ceded the former kingdom of the Isles to Alexander in return for 1,000 marks a year for four years and 100 marks a year in perpetuity. It was also declared that the people of Man and the Isles were to be subject to the laws and customs of the realm of Scotland. This undoubtedly marked the end of what was left of the somewhat nebulous kingdom of the Isles, but not, as we shall see, of the emerging concept of a kingdom of Man.

Chapter Six
Man under Scottish and English Lords, 1266-1405

SCOTTISH RULE, 1266-1333

What was the Isle of Man like in 1266? It was a Christian community strongly linked to the Church of Rome and there was a cathedral on St Patrick's Isle as well as some sort of fortified residence for the kings. Towards the end of the previous century some sixteen or seventeen parishes had been established, each with a parish church and several smaller keeills, and the bishop had a residence at Kirk Michael. There was a small Cistercian abbey at Rushen and a fortified castle nearby. There were certainly no towns and there is no evidence even for villages. Homesteads were isolated and based upon the 700 or so quarterland farms and the houses were by now of the Norse, rectangular type, though generally small. Most of the islanders survived by farming and fishing when they were not fighting. There were no baronial castles or manor houses because feudalism had not been introduced: there was a less hierarchical and more 'democratic' Scandinavian social and legal system and there were freemen and 'slaves'. The chief freemen (later the 'Keys') advised the king at meetings of Tynwald, where laws affecting the whole community were announced. There were almost certainly two spoken languages in use, the original Gaelic as well as Norse, because many Vikings had married Island girls and the mother tongue prevailed. In fact as the Scandinavian connection with Man began to disappear, so did the Norse language, leaving Gaelic to predominate. A handful of scholars and churchmen, of course, could read and write Latin. The population probably numbered only a few thousand.

All this did not really amount to very much, yet as the history of the next 150 years makes clear the Isle of Man, even shorn of its island empire, was still a very desirable prize. This was partly because of its usefulness as a staging-post in the Irish Sea but largely because of its historic associations and the prestige of the royal crown associated with its ruler. For instance, Alexander III conferred upon his son and heir the title 'Lord of Man', rather in the way that Edward

I of England later created his eldest son 'Prince of Wales'. However, the Manx were not disposed to accept the Treaty of Perth without resistance and in 1275 they rebelled against Scottish rule under the leadership of the late King Magnus' illegitimate son Godred, who captured Castle Rushen and sent the Scots packing. This resulted in an interdict imposed on the rebels by Bishop Mark of Sodor and a Scottish army landed in October and forced Godred to flee to Wales, having lost 537 supporters killed in battle.

The Manx kept quiet after this but the Scottish royal house of Stewart went into crisis during the 1280s with the death of Alexander's three children. When he himself died in 1286 his heir was his young grand-daughter Margaret but she, too, died in 1290. Scottish law permitted illegitimate children born in Scotland to claim an inheritance and also those descended from the female line, so twelve individuals claimed the Scottish throne. In these exceptional circumstances the Scots agreed to recognize Edward I of England as their 'superior lord' and gave to him the task of judging who should be king in Scotland. He chose John Balliol, who was duly installed, though not before doing homage to Edward, which many Scots strongly resented.

Alexander's death in 1286 prompted two people to lay claim to the kingdom of Man. One was John Waldeboeuf who had married Mary, the widow of King Magnus, and the other was Affreca of Connaught, apparently a cousin of Magnus. They were both upstaged by Richard de Burgh, Earl of Ulster, who took control of the Island, probably on the orders of Edward I. An assembly of islanders met at Rushen Abbey and asked for Edward I's protection in a document authorized by their common seal. Edward granted this protection in 1290 and appointed Walter de Huntercombe as custodian of the Island. This was undoubtedly a violation of the rights of the Scottish royal house but it seems that Edward wanted lead from the Island's mines for the building of his ring of new castles in Wales. After he had judged John Balliol to be King of Scotland in 1292, he handed control of the Island back to him the following year.

In 1296 Balliol, under pressure from the Scottish lords, renounced his allegiance to Edward who then marched north with the intention of conquering Scotland as he had recently conquered Wales. He routed Balliol at Dunbar, deposed him, and dispatched the symbolic Stone of Scone, upon which Scottish kings had been crowned for centuries, to Westminster. Bishop Mark of Sodor was summoned to do homage to Edward at Dumfries but must have resisted because he and the bishop of Glasgow were in 1299 believed by Pope Boniface VIII to be in prison. It seems that the Isle of Man was 'conquered' from the Scots by the English nobles Simon Montacute and his son William, who may have 'mortgaged' it to Antony Bek, bishop of Durham, who assumed control in 1301, styling himself 'Lord of Man'. After he died in 1311 Edward II possibly granted the Island briefly to his close friend Piers Gaveston and then to his supporter Henry de Beaumont 'with all its dominion and royal rights, together with knight's fees, advowsons of churches and religious houses, liberties, free customs, escheats and all other of its appurtenances…'

However, the English attempt to subdue Scotland was running out of steam. The Scots rallied round a new king, Robert Bruce, in 1306, and Edward I died in the following year leaving the throne to his far less capable son Edward II. In 1312 the Scots and Norwegians renewed the Treaty of Perth and in 1313 Robert of Scotland personally led an attack on the Isle of Man. He landed with a considerable force at Ramsey on May 18th, spent a night at the nunnery in Douglas and then laid siege to Castle Rushen, held for Henry de Beaumont by Duncan MacDowell, who may have been a personal enemy of King Robert. MacDowell put up strong resistance but the castle fell after a month and was demolished by the victorious Scots. The following year Edward II's invasion of Scotland resulted in disaster when Bruce destroyed his army at Bannockburn.

Despite this, the Isle of Man was recovered from the Scots by John of Argyll, the admiral of Edward II's Irish Sea fleet, who may have repaired Castle Rushen to some extent and used it as a base for his operations. In 1316 Robert of Scotland granted the Lordship of Man to his follower the Earl of Moray and left him to conquer the Island, which he managed to do the following year. In 1323 the English and Scots made a truce and in 1324 Robert of Scotland granted Moray a new charter styling him not Lord, but King of Man, with enjoyment of practically all powers except the appointment of the bishop. For a short period, there was quiet on the Island until Moray's death in Scotland in 1332.

THE MONTACUTES AND THEIR SUCCESSORS, 1333-1405

By 1332 the English throne was again in the hands of an able young ruler, Edward III, who was determined to complete his grandfather's unfinished business by defeating the Scots, which he managed to do

William de Montacute, second Earl of Salisbury, with his Countess. Notice that he wears the three legs of Man on his surcoat and a coronet upon his head. (Manx National Heritage)

in both 1332 and 1333. As part of this campaign he sent ships from Bristol which captured the Isle of Man and in August he renounced all personal and dynastic claims to the Island and, ignoring the rights of Moray's heir, he bestowed it upon his closest friend and ally, William, Lord Montacute. William and his father Simon had laid claim to the Island for many years on the grounds that they had 'conquered' it about 1300 and also because Affreca of Connaught had transferred her claims to them, possibly through marriage. Montacute was also created Earl of Salisbury in 1337 and seems to have established his hold on Man by force of arms in the early 1340s, when according to the English chronicler Geoffrey le Baker, he was actually crowned king on the Island, though both he and his son generally used the title 'Lord'. The Scots were still capable of raiding in the Irish Sea and Montacute was himself much involved with Edward III's attempt to conquer France, which had begun in 1340, so there was little security on the Island until 1346 when King David of Scotland was captured at the battle of Neville's Cross and taken prisoner.

The first Earl of Salisbury died in 1344 as a result of wounds suffered in a tournament at Windsor, leaving a boy of sixteen, also named William, as his heir. He had none of his father's military or diplomatic abilities and did not retain the high favour of Edward III, but he founded a Franciscan friary at Bymaken, Ballabeg, and it was during his time that Rushen Castle was reconstructed with a formidable stone keep, curtain wall and gateway. In 1348 western Europe was devasted by the 'Black Death' which killed a third of the population, and although there is no specific evidence for its effects on Man, there is no reason to suppose that the Island, so closely linked to the surrounding area by sea traffic, would have escaped. In 1378 the 'Great Schism' complicated affairs in the Roman Church when two rival popes were elected, one in Rome and one based in Avignon, and rulers everywhere were forced to choose which one to recognize. England eventually recognized Rome while Scotland accepted Avignon, and Bishop John Donkan in the Isle of Man followed Edward III in recognizing the pope in Rome, as a result of which the pope in Avignon deposed him and appointed a bishop of Sodor for the Western Isles. After this, though the Manx bishop retained the title 'Sodor and Man', his authority lay in the Island only.

In 1392, after an exceptionally long and (as far as we know) fairly peaceful reign of 48 years, the second Earl of Salisbury sold the Isle of Man to Sir William Scrope for a large sum of money - 10,000 marks. Why he did this at a time when the Island had formally been recognized by both the kings of England and Scotland as an autonomous lordship with accepted claims to royal status is not clear. Perhaps Salisbury needed the money and, having no son, was not concerned about a hereditary succession. Scrope made himself indispensable to Richard II and was one of the most hated men in England, disliked for being ruthless and ambitious. Not surprisingly, he made full use of the title 'King of Man' and he encouraged Richard in his dangerous policy of attempting to create an 'absolute' monarchy in England, and in his disinheritance of his cousin Henry, heir to the dukedom of Lancaster. Another of Richard's targets was his enemy Thomas Beauchamp, Earl of Warwick, who was handed over to Scrope in 1397 for imprisonment in Peel Castle, where Scrope had been responsible for new fortifications as well as repairs to the cathedral. In 1399 Richard's regime was swept away by Henry of Lancaster who rebelled and deposed him and took the throne as Henry IV. Scrope, recently ennobled by Richard as Earl of Wiltshire, was one of the first to be executed in Bristol as a traitor.

Scrope's English possessions were declared forfeit to the Crown but in recognition of the Isle of Man's special status it was deemed to be conquered territory. Henry passed it on without delay to his chief supporter Henry Percy, Earl of Northumberland, but he did not keep it long because within a few years he became dissatisfied with Henry's rule and rebelled. The king defeated his rebellion and in the summer of 1405 Northumberland's lands were declared forfeit and Sir John Stanley was authorized to take control of the Isle of Man and hold it until given further orders.

The years from 1333 to 1405 on the Island are not well documented, partly because the 'Chronicles of the Kings of Man and the Isles' end the main story in 1316 with an account of a raid on the Island by Irish marauders led by Richard de Mandeville, though some authorities think this might actually have occurred in 1337. Moreover the records of the Montacute family have not been well preserved. We have no evidence that either of the Montacutes, or Scrope, or Northumberland ever visited the Island, which was governed by various of their appointed representatives. The celebrated French writer Jean Froissart knew just enough about the Island to feature it in his epic poem 'Meliador', and the chivalric Catalan hero Ramon de Pelleros claimed to have visited the Island in 1397 and considered it well populated. Beyond that and the knowledge that both Rushen Castle and Peel Castle were considerably strengthened and extended, we know little in detail except that the Island and its royal lordship survived these years of conflict, plague and confusion to enter upon a more settled phase under the control of Sir John Stanley and his heirs.

Chapter Seven
The Early Stanleys, 1406-1504

On April 6th 1406 Henry IV rewarded Sir John Stanley for his loyalty with a formal grant to him of the Isle of Man in return for the surrender of a previous grant of 100 marks for life. The grant of the Island was in perpetuity with the requirement to provide two falcons at the coronation of Henry's successors and it included all the traditional prerogatives of the Island's kings as well as the right to appoint the bishop and parish priests. Stanley was born about 1350, the younger son of William Stanley of Storeton in Cheshire, who as bailiff of the forest of Wirral was notorious for his oppressive tactics. As a very young man John Stanley fought in the campaigns against France but he was outlawed in 1376 for his part in the murder of one Thomas Clotton. Pardoned in 1378 he fought again in France, hopeful of achieving fame and fortune as a knight. By 1385 he had succeeded sufficiently in this aim to win the hand in marriage of Isabel, the heiress of Sir Thomas Lathom of Lathom and Knowsley, two estates in south-west Lancashire. In 1386 he became deputy to Robert de Vere, Richard II's favourite whom he had appointed Duke of Ireland, and from 1389 to 1391 he served as Justiciar of Ireland. He supported Richard II throughout the 1390s, reaching the heart of the royal court as controller of the wardrobe in 1397.

Stanley accompanied Richard II on his ill-advised expedition to Ireland in 1399, which gave the banished Henry of Lancaster his chance to strike against the king while he was overseas. Returning to find Lancaster in control of much of the country, Stanley submitted to him in August 1399, thereby betraying Richard but winning the gratitude of Lancaster when he usurped the throne as Henry IV. He was granted the lordships of Mold and Hope in North Wales and served as Lieutenant in Ireland. In 1403 he became steward to the household of Henry, Prince of Wales and remained loyal to Henry IV during the rebellion of Northumberland that year, fighting fiercely at the battle of Shrewsbury where he was wounded in the throat. About the same time as he was granted the Isle of Man in 1406 he became steward of the king's household and a knight of the Garter and in 1409

Castle Rushen. By the 15th century the main keep and curtain walls were complete but 'Ca

ot established until the end of the century. (Manx National Heritage)

he was made constable of Windsor Castle. After the accession of his former protégé the Prince of Wales as Henry V he was again made Lieutenant of Ireland where local chroniclers regarded him as ruthless and grasping. He died in 1414 at Ardee, in Louth, from a Bardic curse, so the Irish claimed.

Sir John Stanley was therefore crucially involved in the turbulent politics of his age and never visited his island kingdom though his son, also named John, came to Man in his father's lifetime and received the faith and fealty of the barons and the worthiest men and commons as heir apparent. There can be little doubt that the first Stanley made good provision for the Island's administration and government because he saw it literally as the crowning achievement in his lifetime's pursuit of power, land and influence in the north-west. This was symbolized to some extent by a crenellated tower which he had erected at Liverpool in 1406 and from where he and his successors supervised much of the administration of the Isle of Man as well as their other estates.

Sir John Stanley II had far less of a national profile than his father but he remained in favour at court and devoted a good deal of his time to the affairs of the Island, which he visited on a number of occasions. The Stanleys probably inherited an administrative structure which included a Governor and four members of the Lord's Council who were the comptroller, the receiver, the water bailiff and the attorney general. They were all appointed by the Lord and their main duties were to maintain his rights and collect the revenue due to him on the Island. Together with the two deemsters they also held law courts in the Lord's name. In addition the Governor was responsible for appointing a chief officer called a coroner in each of the six sheadings as well as his assistants, called lockmen, in each parish. He also appointed captains of the parishes to organize local militias.

The precise way in which Tynwald functioned at this time and the role of the Keys are both difficult to pin down. There can be little doubt that, as has been explained, Tynwald had its origins in the tenth century as part of the Scandinavian method of government imported into the Island and the Keys probably date from that time also, but the documentary evidence illustrating how the mechanisms worked is lacking. Olaf I's grant of land at Rushen to Furness Abbey in 1134 states that he took this decision having consulted the people and with the counsel and consent of the wise and the worthy. Tynwald is mentioned by the Chronicle as the place where the battle of St Valentine's Day took place in 1228, and in 1237 it describes how 'an assembly of the entire Manx populace was held at Tynwald'.

Further light is cast on the workings of Tynwald in the time of the second Sir John Stanley who was prompted to visit the Island in 1417 because there had been a revolt against his Governor, John Letherland. This he suppressed and the Tynwald Court advised him that the rebels were legally liable to be hanged, drawn and quartered. In 1422 there was another attack on the Governor, John Walton, while he was sitting in court at Kirk Michael. Stanley came to the Island again and summoned a special Tynwald Court to meet him at Reneurling Hill, (Cronk Urley), on August 22nd. The culprits were sentenced to death, subject to the Lord's pardon. On this occasion the bishop did homage and the laws were confirmed by 'Sir John Stanley, by the Grace of God, King of Man and the Isles, and by the best of the Commons of the Isle of Man'. Also in this year the deemsters told Stanley that the origin of the Keys was uncertain but in what they termed 'King Orry's days' the Keys, whom they described as 'Taxiaxi', were 24 freeholders – eight in the 'Out Isles' and sixteen in 'your land of Man'. Much ink has been spilled over the precise meaning of this but it is now thought that sixteen of the members represented the sixteen original early twelfth century parishes of the Island and the remaining eight were added after the loss of the Hebrides and Skye in 1266. With twenty-four members, the Keys became based not on the 16 parishes but on the six sheadings, drawing four men from each. It is likely that until after 1600 the Keys were not a permanent body but were called when required by the deemsters, choosing from the worthiest men in the Island. Why they are called 'Keys' is the final conundrum, with various theories being advanced, one of which is that the Manx for 'the four and twenty' is 'Yn Kiare as feed' and 'The Keys' is an attempt to render this in English.

Sir John Stanley was clearly not sure how things stood because in 1423 he summoned the two deemsters and twenty-four Keys to Castle Rushen on March 24th in order to discover from them exactly what they considered the Island's ancient constitution to be and how it worked in practice. In 1429 the Governor, Henry Byron, presided over a Tynwald Court which abolished trial by combat and replaced it with trial by jury. It also determined that no man's goods should be taken except by process of law and that a husband was liable for a wife's debts. At the same time uniformity of weights and measures was established.

The biggest challenge to the authority of the Stanleys on the Island was the Church. The completion of the cathedral at Peel about 1250 made it by far the most impressive building on the Island and the bishop lived in some style on the Bishopscourt site, especially after the construction of a three storey peel tower there in the next century. As a result of the schism in the papacy bishops appointed after John Donkan left in 1392 were no longer in effect bishops of Sodor as well as Man (though the title has obstinately lingered to this day) and this meant that they were more likely to be resident on the Island and to concern themselves in detail with its affairs, in particular the levying of tithes and other church taxes. These were never popular, especially the tithe introduced on the herring fishery by Bishop Thomas (1334-1348). The second most important church dignitary was the Abbot of Rushen, who, like the bishop, was one of the Island's six ecclesiastical barons. He controlled the abbey's considerable estates and was inevitably an influential figure, especially in the south of the Island. The other four baronies were those of the priory of Douglas, in Braddan, the priory of St Bee's (Cumberland), in Maughold, the barony of the abbeys of Bangor and Sabal (Ireland), in Patrick, and the barony of St Trinian's in German and Marown, which belonged to the priory of Whithorn in Galloway.

Like his father Sir John Stanley II was a Lollard - a follower of the English church reformer John Wycliffe - and from the outset he was determined to reduce the authority of the Island's ecclesiastical dignitaries. Soon after his visit to the Island in 1417 the deemsters, at his instigation, declared the right of sanctuary to be abolished, which meant that felons could not escape civil punishment by handing themselves over to the Church. In 1422 the bishop and ecclesiastical barons were forbidden to take more than £5 out of the Island, or to receive strangers without the knowledge of the Governor, and at the meeting of Tynwald at Reneurling Hill already mentioned all the six barons were required to do fealty in person to Sir John as Lord. The bishop, the Abbot of Rushen and the Prioress of Douglas attended but the Abbots of Furness, Bangor and Sabal as well as the Priors of Whithorn and St Bee's did not and the deemsters ruled that if they failed to attend in person within forty days they would forfeit their temporal rights. In 1429 the Lord's authority over the bishop was emphasized when a jury of 24 men impanelled by the deemsters upheld an appeal against a sentence imposed by the bishop's officials.

In these ways Stanley increased the Lord's grip on the Island and brought it peace and a measure of security seldom known in the past.

There were still no towns until the end of the century and the Island remained an essentially agricultural community, perhaps numbering up to 10,000 people, nearly all of whom spoke only Manx Gaelic. The Manx 'serf' had probably made the transition to being a free labourer early in the fourteenth century and by 1422 it is likely that he was earning enough to make a frugal living and he was protected from arrest for debt or any other crime unless tried by the deemsters according to due legal process. His social status was low and he was subject to being 'yarded' - or taken from his current master and required to serve the Lord and his chief officers for a nominal wage. Also, a law of 1422 ordained that no Manxman who had sworn fealty to the Lord could leave the Island without permission and aliens could not live in the Island unless they swore fealty. At this time, and for many years to come, the value of external trade to the Island does not seem to have been appreciated and it was discouraged by complicated regulations.

On the death of Sir John Stanley II in 1437 his son Thomas succeeded to the Stanley estates and the lordship of Man at the age of 31. He married Joan Goushill in 1422, which made him the brother-in-law of the Duke of Norfolk and Lord Berkeley, he represented Lancashire in Parliament in 1427 and in 1431 he was appointed Lieutenant of Ireland. By 1439 he was controller of the household to the boy king Henry VI and a member of the clique of lords who ruled England in his name. As Henry VI grew to manhood and proved to be a weak ruler his position was challenged by his cousin the Duke of York in 1455 and a series a battles took place between the followers of King Henry (the Lancastrians), and the Yorkists, leading to the deposition of Henry and the accession of York as Edward IV in 1461. Throughout these tortuous events Stanley played a very clever diplomatic game, always seeming to end up on the winning side, and he was created a peer as Lord Stanley in 1455 and made a knight of the Garter in 1457. He died in February 1459 just as these 'Wars of the Roses' moved into another active phase.

Stanley left two sons, his successor Thomas, the second Lord Stanley, and his brother Sir William. Born in 1433 Thomas made a grand marriage in the late 1450s to Eleanor, daughter of Richard Neville, Earl of Salisbury, and sister of Richard Neville, Earl of Warwick. Within months of his father's death Stanley found himself in a dangerous situation because Queen Margaret (who was the driving force behind her husband Henry VI) ordered him to intercept the rebel

89

troops of his Yorkist father-in-law the Earl of Salisbury, which included his own brother William. When Margaret met Salisbury in battle at Bloreheath in August 1459 Stanley kept his 2,000 men out of the fighting and managed to secure a pardon from the Queen afterwards for this act of disloyalty. However, as the power-scale tipped towards the Yorkists he joined them before the proclamation of Edward of York as king in 1461. Stanley survived the quarrel between the king and his own brother-in-law the Earl of Warwick in 1470 and 1471 and during the 1470s he was a regular member of the royal council. In 1472, after the death of his first wife, he married the widowed Margaret Beaufort, Countess of Richmond. She was directly descended from Edward III, which meant that Henry Tudor, her son by her former husband, had a strong claim to the throne. Stanley accompanied Edward IV on campaign in France in 1475 and assisted royal forces to capture Berwick in an attack on Scotland in 1482.

When Edward IV died suddenly in 1483 he left his twelve-year-old son to succeed him as Edward V. His uncle Richard of Gloucester, named as Protector of the Realm, felt threatened by the young king's mother and her many brothers and declared Edward illegitimate and proclaimed himself king as Richard III. He decided he needed the support of Stanley and offered him friendship and influence at Court and appointed him a knight of the Garter. When Richard was faced with a major rebellion in 1483 Stanley supported him and he was rewarded with the office of constable of England and some of the estates of defeated rebels. In 1485, however, Stanley's stepson Henry Tudor invaded England with a Lancastrian force and marched to do battle with the Yorkist Richard at Bosworth, in Leicestershire, leaving Stanley in the difficult position of having to decide whom he should support - his king or his wife's son. He took his personal army of about 5000 men to the battlefield, as did his brother William, but Stanley's men, as at Bloreheath, stood by and did nothing, while his brother's men actually attacked Richard III, leading directly to his death. Tradition insists that as Richard's body fell, his royal coronet rolled from his helmet and either Lord Stanley or his brother Sir William placed it on Henry Tudor's head, hailing him as king. If it was Lord Stanley who did this, it could be reasonably claimed that a King of Man had, in a historic role-reversal, created a King of England.

The new king promptly rewarded Lord Stanley by granting him the earldom of Derby on October 27th 1485 and confirming him as Constable of England and High Steward of the Duchy of Lancaster. The

Thomas, second Lord Stanley and first Earl of Derby. (Manx National Heritage)

Engraved by W. Holl.

Derby of the title was the county town of Derbyshire and the earldom was an ancient one which had reverted to the Crown through lack of heirs. However, it was recognized at the time to be a particularly appropriate title in this case because the centre of the Stanley estates was situated in the Lancashire hundred of Derby (now West Derby, near Liverpool). Derby supported Henry in his battle against rebels at Stoke in 1487 and received yet more estates in Lancashire as a reward but his brother William foolishly supported the Perkin Warbeck rebellion in 1495 and was executed for treason. Derby died in 1504 having played a major part in national events for more than forty years. During this time he steadily increased the power and prestige of his family in Lancashire and Cheshire and stepped skilfully around the obstacles of civil war. His success in this meant that the north-west of England was spared excessive damage during this restless period while the Isle of Man escaped more or less unscathed. Had Derby placed himself on the losing side in any of the many political conflicts through which he lived, the Island might well have gone as spoil to the victors and its steady development might have been seriously disrupted.

There are few Island records for the second half of the fifteenth century except for the Book of the Statutes which reveals that the main interest of the Lord's officers was the preservation of his various rights and privileges, such as the right to take all catches of porpoise, sturgeon and whale - all considered 'royal' fish - as well as game such as hawk, heron, hart and hind. He was also entitled to free food for the garrisons of Castle Rushen and Peel Castle, with each quarterland having the obligation to provide one beef a year. Corn and herring were also due to him for this purpose, while treasure trove, wrecked ships and their contents and the goods of all people condemned to death were also his. A tax had to be paid for the right to fish for herring and for the right to grind flour at the Lord's mills. Many tried to avoid this by using hand mills, which was an offence. All men between the ages of twenty and sixty were required to do compulsory military training under the command of the captains of the parishes, using bows and arrows and sword and buckler, all of which they had to provide themselves. Almost every man was required to carry out the ancient duty of keeping 'watch and ward' by day and night at the time-hallowed watch stations across the Island ('Barrule' means 'look-out hill' in Manx) and there were severe penalties for failing in this obligation. There were detailed rules about the hiring of farm labourers and servants of both sexes and whipping was the penalty for those who failed in their duties. Parents who were elderly or ill were allowed to keep one of their adult children at home to look after them.

The Lord's Governor was responsible for the day-to-day running of the Island, assisted by his administrative officials, while the two deemsters made sure the laws were obeyed. It seems that no new laws were passed between 1430 and 1504 and the Keys during this period were little more than a supreme jury called infrequently to deal with exceptional issues. Although the Stanley Lords rarely visited the Island they were served by an efficient and able team of administrators in England, and from their bases at the Tower in Liverpool and their houses at Lathom and Knowsley they kept a close watch on the Island and in particular the revenues due from it to them. Around 1507 a major administrative advance was made with the introduction of the 'Setting Books' which contained the names of all landowners and the rent owed by them to the Lord. Also the 'Wast Books', dating from 1511, recorded the admissions, entries and titles of of landowners and the alienation fines and rents paid to them. These records were maintained until 1911 and 1916 respectively and can still be vitally important for legal searches.

The turn of the century was probably about the time when the Manx Traditionary Ballad, or Manannan Ballad, was first written down. With subsequent additions and omissions it now consists of 62 quatrains in Manx Gaelic, mostly in iambic pentameter. In translation the first quatrain asks

> Would you have patience for a chant?
> Could my weak words your thoughts beguile?
> Well, if attention you would grant,
> I'd sing you a song of the Blessed Isle.

The Ballad then recounts many colourful episodes from Manx tradition and history and as such it is a significant historical source. Its main importance, however, is linguistic because it is thought that the first 57 quatrains date from about 1500, which is earlier than any other surviving text in Manx Gaelic.

Chapter Eight
The Stanleys and the Tudors

T he first Earl of Derby's son George was born about 1460 and he married Joan Strange, who was the heir to the ancient barony of Strange of Knockin, a title often used in future by eldest sons of the Earls of Derby. However, George Stanley died before his father, so his son Thomas succeeded as the second earl and as Lord of Man in 1504. Thomas married Anne Hastings and in 1507 he led an attack on the Scots in Kircudbrightshire, after which he sailed to the Isle of Man, landing at Ronaldsway in May. Ballads describe enthusiastically the magnificence of his household, the number of his servants and his golden attire. His descendant the seventh earl claimed that it was Thomas who decided not to be called 'King of Man', preferring the lesser title 'Lord', but since the thirteenth century the title of King of Man had been very rarely used outside the Island by the Scottish or English aristocrats who had been granted it, for the good reason that it appeared pretentious. This was especially, and dangerously, the case at the court of Henry VIII, who could be lethally jealous of overmighty subjects. So from about this time the title 'Lord of Man' was generally (but not always) used in the Island as well.

Henry VII had proved to be one of the most able of all English kings and he ended the civil wars which had weakened the nation for more than fifty years. He also reduced the power of the nobles, increased the authority of the Crown and amassed a vast fortune in the royal treasury. His eighteen-year-old son Henry VIII succeeded him in 1509 and set out to be a flamboyant 'Renaissance Prince', well versed in love, literature, music and war and just as determined as his father had been to maintain the power and authority of the Tudor dynasty. Earl Thomas accompanied Henry on his successful campaign to France in 1513, fighting at the battle of the Spurs, but the following year it seems that he offended the King by high-handed behaviour in the north-west, such as his unauthorized interference in the affairs of the Abbey of Furness. He recovered from this setback and was made a member of the Privy Council in 1520, though he died the following

Thomas, second Earl of Derby. (Courtesy of the Rt Hon. The Earl of Derby 2007)

year, probably only in his late thirties.

His son Edward, the third earl, was only eleven when his father died, a potentially disastrous situation for noble families because the custom was for the young heir to become the ward of another influential noble until he reached the age of 21. This often meant that the ward's estates and revenues were drained by the noble in charge of him. Edward became the ward of Henry VIII's ruthless and avaricious, though exceptionally able, minister Cardinal Thomas Wolsey, who for the next nine years made free use of the vast Derby estates, allegedly extracting from them the enormous sum of £5,500. Wolsey died in 1530 but Edward was still only twenty and the last year of his wardship was purchased by the Duke of Norfolk who insisted on his marriage to his daughter Katherine. When she died only months later Norfolk then insisted that he should marry his sister Dorothy, so determined was he to keep the Derby connection within the family. This marriage seemed to work well enough, producing three sons and four daughters. When Dorothy died Edward married again, fathering another son and two daughters.

Earl Edward came into his inheritance in 1531 and had to begin a long process of restructuring his finances and raising capital by increasing rents. He was with Henry VIII when he met Francis I of France at the 'Field of the Cloth of Gold' in 1532 and became a knight of the Bath in 1533, acting as cup-bearer at the coronation of Anne Boleyn. In 1538 the Pope was informed in a report that Derby was 'the greatest of power and land' among the English nobility, but also that he was 'young, and a child in wisdom, and half a fool'. Nevertheless, he had many important responsibilities in the north-west, not least in regard to its security, and he took steps to ensure that the Isle of Man should be protected. Scotland was still an ancient enemy whose main army had been crushed for the time being by a defeat at Flodden in 1513 but Scottish raids on the Island were still a real possibility. Derby maintained garrisons of at least 35 men at Castle Rushen and at Peel and in 1533 he sent 40 archers to the Island from Lancashire and a force of a hundred men in 1540. Between 1538 and 1540 he ordered that small round forts should be built on Pollock Rock at Douglas and on St Michael's Island outside Derbyhaven and an earthen fort was constructed on the northern plain at Ballachurry.

The 1530s were among the most momentous decades in English history because during this period Henry VIII, forced into a corner by

Edward, third Earl of Derby. (Manx National Heritage)

the Pope's refusal to annul his first marriage, took the dramatic step of breaking away from the authority of the Pope and effectively became Head of the English Church himself. As such he then decided to close down all the English monasteries on the grounds that the monks were too rich, lazy and unpopular. The large monastic houses were the first to go in 1536 and this led to many protests and one serious rebellion in the north, known as the Pilgrimage of Grace, which the King dealt with in typically ruthless fashion. By 1539 all the rest of the monasteries were closed and a major social and religious revolution had been accomplished in England. In 1541, mirroring the fact that the King was Head of the Church in England, Derby was declared to be Metropolitan and Chief of the Holy Church on the Island.

There is no doubt that some features of the Church were as much resented on the Island as they were in Britain. In 1532 complaints had reached Derby from the Isle of Man that the Church was charging heavy and unwarranted taxes on death dues, tithes on brewing ale and marriage presents, and bishop's fees. Derby appointed a commission to look into this matter, chaired by the Governor, John Fleming, and it greatly reduced many church fees and abolished the tithes on ale and on marriage presents. After the first group of large monasteries were closed in England, many wondered what would happen to the monasteries on the Island. Furness Abbey was dissolved in 1537 and the tithes due to it from its barony in Maughold and Michael seemingly went straight to the king and not to Derby. The Act of 1539 which dissolved the lesser English monasteries did not specifically mention the Island and therefore did not apply to it, and no law for the dissolution of the Manx monasteries was passed by the Island authorities. Nevertheless Rushen Abbey, the nunnery at Douglas and the friary at Bymaken were all closed, apparently on the sole authority of the king.

On St John the Baptist's Day, 1540, the abbot and the six monks of Rushen were required to leave, as was the prioress of Douglas and her three nuns. Their tithes went to the king, but when Whithorn priory was dissolved some time later, its tithes in Marown and Lezayre went to Derby, while the tithes due to Bangor, Sabal and St Bee's found their way into private hands. Henry VIII's lack of regard for the rights of the Lord of Man on this issue, though typical of his brand of 'Tudor despotism', is illuminating. In fact King James I restored all the main tithes to the sixth Earl of Derby in 1609, but that was of no comfort to the third earl. Meanwhile the monastic church and buildings at Rushen fell into disuse and gradual decay. It is likely that the closure of the abbey was some loss to the poor of the Island and it left the bishop as the only remaining spiritual baron, cut off from the support-systems of the international Roman Church.

Henry VIII died in 1547, in his own view still a Catholic, but under his nine-year-old son Edward VI the Protestant Reformation took hold in England and Acts of Parliament made fundamental changes to traditional Catholic beliefs. It is clear that Derby was marked down by the new regime as a dangerous traditionalist, and his autonomous control of the Isle of Man was seen as a threat because a papal report of 1550 claimed that he had been required to renounce his title to the Island and had refused, saying that he would resist by force. Two powerful nobles, the Duke of Somerset and the Earl of Warwick, competed for control over the young king, and Derby had to tread warily through yet another minefield of political intrigue, as did his son Henry, Lord Strange. When the king died in 1553 aged only sixteen, Derby supported the accession of Henry VIII's Catholic daughter Mary and returned to the centre of government as a privy councillor. Sir Thomas Wyatt led a rebellion against Mary and this time Derby helped to defeat him and was regarded as particularly remarkable among the nobility because of his great popular following. Elizabeth I succeeded her sister in 1558 and gradually brought England back to the Protestant fold. Because of his well-known Catholic sympathies Elizabeth did not really trust Derby but he remained a privy councillor and did not take part in a Catholic rebellion led by northern noblemen in 1569, though his younger sons Edward and Thomas were implicated in plots to support the Catholic heir, Mary Queen of Scots.

Earl Edward managed to die in his bed at Lathom House on October 24th, 1572, aged 63, and a magnificent funeral service followed in Ormskirk parish church, where a chapel and monumental tomb were built in his memory. Considered while a young man as 'half a fool', he was described even as late as 1567 in diplomatic correspondence as 'not so prudent as potent', which was not flattering. Yet he held on to his great position and his estates through perilous times, his houses were regarded as centres of local culture and he was considered lavish in his hospitality, reputedly feeding sixty poor people every day and 2700 on Good Friday. His lack of enthusiasm for the Protestant Reformation meant, as his opponents had feared, that he made little attempt to encourage the new religion in the north-west, and especially in the Isle of Man. English clergy were allowed to marry in 1549, but Manx clergy could not do so until 1610. Requiems for the dead were still being said on the Island in 1594 and bells and banners were carried before the corpse. England had been provided, by statute, with new Protestant prayer books but in the Island comparatively few people could even speak, let alone read English.

It is difficult to say when and how Protestantism was introduced to the Island, but the first resident Protestant priest seems to have been Thomas Allen who came to Castletown in the 1550s, a refugee from the Catholic regime of Queen Mary. Nor is it known who was appointed the first Protestant vicar on the Island, or when, though it is thought that Sir John Christian was the first Protestant vicar of Maughold from 1580. Neither Bishop John Meyrick (1576-1599) nor his Archdeacon were enthusiastic reformers and both were frequently absent in England tending to other duties. Bishop John Phillips (1604-1633) completed a Manx version of the Book of Common Prayer in 1611, but it was not actually printed until 1893. In 1633 Archbishop Laud was told that of the fifteen priests in Man all except two or three were illiterate men brought up on the Island.

QUEEN ELIZABETH I BECOMES LORD OF MAN

Earl Edward was succeeded by his son Henry, the fourth earl, aged 41. In his youth he had been a close companion of the boy king Edward VI and had been educated in Protestant circles. In February 1555 he was married in the Chapel Royal to Margaret Clifford and this became an extremely significant union because Margaret was the grand-daughter of Henry VIII's younger sister Mary. As the years wore on and Tudor heirs died out or were executed she became second in line to the throne. She bore her husband four sons, two of whom, Ferdinando and William, survived, but she quarrelled with him a great deal and they eventually separated in 1567, after which he made a common law marriage to a local woman, by whom he had several children. What he did share with Margaret was a love of literature, music and drama and he was the patron of a company of actors who performed in his houses.

Although his father had been criticized by diplomats for imprudent behaviour, it was really Henry who lacked wisdom, in financial matters at least. His father, aware of his shortcomings, left many of

Henry, fourth Earl of Derby. (Manx National Heritage)

his estates in trust so that Henry could not dispose of them to redeem his debts, which were a problem throughout his life. Like his father he maintained a princely lifestyle, keeping as many as 145 household staff and taking large retinues abroad when Queen Elizabeth entrusted him with a number of foreign embassies. His wife, whom he was required to maintain for life, was a serial spendthrift whose debts became a major embarrassment and at various times Henry came close to insolvency. He attempted to recoup money by enclosing many of his estates in the north-west and letting them out at higher rents and he visited the Isle of Man in 1577 and 1585 with a view to improving his rents from the Island. He found the 'tenure

101

of straw', which was very advantageous to the tenant, difficult to overcome and in any case the value of his Manx estates was small compared with his holdings in England. According to Bishop Meyrick most of his annual Manx revenue was spent on the administration of the Island. He presided at a common-law court and at a Tynwald Court at St John's on his visit in 1577 and on that occasion the bishop did homage to him for his barony. In 1583 he presided over another Tynwald Court when regulations were passed concerning trout and salmon fishing and in 1585 he asked the deemsters to confirm that any treasure found on the Island was the property of the Lord. In 1592 he appointed his second son William as Governor of the Island, though he only held the post for a short time

Earl Henry died at Lathom House in September 1593 surrounded by debts and in what was described by contemporaries as a violent sea of vomit so putrid that no-one would go near his body until his burial. His successor was his elder son, given the distinctly un-British name Ferdinando, who became the fifth earl in his early thirties. As Lord Strange he had been a protégé of Queen Elizabeth who was partial to handsome young men and who had summoned him to her Court when he was a teenager. He was groomed in good manners and in 1580 he married Alice, daughter of Sir John Spencer of Althorp. He proved to be keen on intellectual pursuits, notably poetry and drama and he ran his own company of actors and tumblers called 'Strange's Men' who performed for the Queen at Court. It is probable that William Shakespeare was a member of this company, several of whom later became part of his acting troupe the 'Lord Chamberlain's Men'. Ferdinando was also a considerable patron of writers and much praised as such. He was not simply an aesthete, however, and served capably while his father was alive as Mayor of Liverpool and as a temporary Lord Lieutenant of Lancashire and Cheshire.

Ferdinando was in many ways the darling of the Court of the ageing and unmarried Elizabeth but he was in a dangerous position politically because of the claim to the throne which he had inherited through his mother. Elizabeth, to the dismay of all her Protestant advisers and subjects, decided not to marry and until 1587 her most likely heir was Mary, the deposed Queen of Scotland, who was a Catholic. The Pope had excommunicated Elizabeth and the King of Spain had undertaken to depose her in favour of Mary with a Spanish army transported by a Spanish fleet. Mary was executed in 1587 after

Ferdinando, fifth Earl of Derby. (Manx National Heritage)

The eastern coastline near Port Soderick. (Miles Cowsill)

being implicated in a plot against Elizabeth and the 'Spanish Armada' was defeated in 1588 by a mixture of good English seamanship, indifferent Spanish leadership, and appalling weather. But the threat of Spanish invasion and Catholic plots was still very real and in the 1590s Elizabeth and her Secretary, William Cecil, (later Lord Burleigh), felt themselves to be surrounded by danger. In 1592 the English ambassador in Edinburgh reported plans for a Franco-Scottish attack on the Isle of Man and in 1595 it was thought that the Catholic Irish, in league with Spain, might invade the Island. Neither Ferdinando nor his younger brother William were Catholics but the risk was that they might become converts and be lured into a plot, dazzled by the prize of the crown. From Cecil's point of view the Stanleys were a risk to national security, being far too rich, far too powerful, and far too close in line to the throne.

Very soon after his father died Ferdinando was indeed approached by Catholic plotters led by Richard Hesketh from Lancashire who encouraged him to make a bid for the crown. Ferdinando lost no time in telling the Queen and Cecil, as a result of which Hesketh was executed. But only a few months after this, Ferdinando himself died in April 1594, aged 35, after suffering agonies of illness for eleven days, following a period of vigorous exercise. Poisoning or witchcraft were suspected and an inquiry was set up into his death, but a modern reading of the symptoms outlined in its report would suggest acute peritonitis.

Ferdinando's sudden death left his widow Alice with three daughters, though no son, and he had made a will which left a large share of the Stanley estates to them. Therefore his bachelor brother William succeeded without dispute to the Derby title as the sixth earl, but there was a legal issue as to whether many of the estates, including the lordship of Man, should pass to William or his 'heirs general', who were his three young daughters. Ferdinando's widow Alice embarked on a determined attempt to claim most of the Stanley lands for herself and her daughters, all of whom were still children, and this began an acrimonious legal contest which was disastrous to the family. Alice was clearly a quarrelsome and greedy woman and her second husband complained bitterly of her biting tongue and constant bad temper and bewailed a marriage full of tempests and storms. On the other hand it is very likely that she was encouraged to pursue prolonged and complicated claims to the Stanley lands by Cecil, so that the family would become burdened with legal fees and debts. Meanwhile Cecil cunningly arranged a marriage between William and his own grand-daughter, Elizabeth de Vere, so that he should have inside information about the family's affairs.

As a result of the legal arguments there was particular uncertainty about who was responsible for the government of the Isle of Man, with Alice disputing with William the right to appoint a new Governor there. This gave Cecil his opportunity to intervene. In 1594 the Attorney General, Edward Coke, formally resumed responsibility for the Island on behalf of the Queen until the argument between Alice and William was resolved in the law courts, on the grounds that a place of such strategic importance must be under undisputed control at such a dangerous time.

Over the heads of William and Alice the Queen appointed Sir Thomas Gerard Governor (technically 'Captain') in August 1595 with orders that he should consider the best means of defending the Island considering that the garrisons of Castle Rushen and Peel Castle were comparatively small. Gerard carried out this commission speedily, recommended the necessary arms and ammunition and moved on to lead a regiment in an attack on Cadiz. He was succeeded as Governor in 1596 by Sir Peter Legh, despite the objections of Earl William. In 1598 the law lords of Elizabeth's Privy Council came to the remarkable conclusion that the grant of the Isle of Man by Henry IV to Sir John Stanley in 1406 was null and void because it had been made before the date of the formal attainder of the Earl of Northumberland, the previous Lord. According to this judgement, all the Stanley Lords of Man had held illegal titles to the Island and it therefore reverted to the Crown. This was a good example of the pragmatic nature of Tudor law and politics in times of national crisis.

Therefore Earl William was formally deprived of the lordship of Man in 1598 and after many further court cases dealing with his dispute with Alice he was required to surrender about a third of his inheritance to her and her daughters and to pay large legal fees so that by 1602 when at last the internal family arguments were resolved, the Earl of Derby was ranked only the 28th richest man in the kingdom. In 1603 Queen Elizabeth died and the succession to the English crown, so long a problematic issue, was resolved quite peacefully by the proclamation of James VI of Scotland as king on the grounds that he was the grandson of Henry VIII's sister Margaret, who had married James V, and that he was therefore the next legitimate heir. Although no formal union took place between the two countries until 1707 (though a 'Union Jack' flag was designed and named after James) they were henceforth ruled by the same royal house. The long-standing contests between England and Scotland, which had impacted on the Isle of Man for centuries, soon came to an end, and as a result the Island ceased to be quite so important strategically.

Chapter Nine
The seventeenth century

James I was famously interested in legal niceties and William and Alice raised again with him the question of their dispossession of the Isle of Man, which they argued had been unjustly decided on a mere technicality. However, in 1607 the king's judges reaffirmed their verdict that the Island belonged to the Crown but pointed out to James that the Stanleys had nevertheless held it for two centuries and left it to the king's own wisdom as to whether the case should be settled according to the letter of the law or according to equitable justice. Considering himself a modern Solomon, James opted for the latter and for the time being put the Island under the control of his Secretary, Robert Cecil, Earl of Salisbury, who was the uncle of William's wife. By 1609 it was agreed that Alice's three daughters should give up their claims to the Island in return for a substantial cash payment and in July 1609 the Island was granted to William and his wife jointly, and to their descendants. The fact that Elizabeth received a half share was probably the work of her uncle, Robert Cecil. The couple became fully responsible for the Island in 1612 and William seems to have left his wife to take charge of it. Though not resident, she showed a keen interest in its affairs and it was she who appointed Governors and to whom petitions were addressed until her death in 1627.

Meanwhile William gave his attention to the consolidation of the rest of his estates and financial affairs, achieving some success in this. But one of his main interests, as with his father and his brother, was the theatre. He kept a troupe of actors known as 'Derby's men' and risked scandal by writing comedies for the London stage towards the end of Elizabeth's reign, which has led to his being included - without foundation - in the list of possible 'Shakespeares'. He was a friend of the poet John Donne and the patron of many literary men. He was also interested in constructing and repairing bridges, in alchemy, and in horse-racing, building stables on the family racecourse at Wallasey.

'THE GREAT STANLEY'?

By the time his wife died in 1627 William, who was then in his mid-sixties, had decided to 'retire' from public affairs and surrender to his reclusive tendencies by living alone in a small house in Chester on a modest income. He formally gave the responsibility of governing the Stanley lands, including the Isle of Man, to his eldest son James, a young man barely twenty. Known as Lord Strange despite the fact that his father had not inherited the barony, James had been educated by private tutors at Lathom and Knowsley and had travelled to France and Italy before becoming MP for Liverpool and then Lord Lieutenant of Lancashire and Cheshire. Early in 1626 he attended the coronation of James I's son, Charles I, and later that year he married Charlotte de la Tremoille, a daughter of the Duc de Thouars and a grand-daughter of the great Protestant hero William, Prince of Orange. The wedding took place in the Hague and was attended by many of Europe's most notable Protestant leaders, including the Elector Palatine.

Closely linked in this way to the Protestant cause, James found that he had little in common with the religious policy favoured in England in the 1630s by Charles I, his Catholic French wife Henrietta Maria and the 'High Church' Archbishop William Laud. He was therefore not a favourite at Court and spent most of the decade at home in Lancashire, rearing his family of six children and administering his estates. His main concern was to restore the family fortunes by efficient management and in the Isle of Man, which he visited during the 1630s, he decided that the existing system of land tenure was not satisfactory to his interests. At the time of Henry IV's grant of the Island to the Stanleys in 1406 it is probable that all the land was regarded as belonging to the Lord and that tenants held it from year to year without any right of inheritance. However over the next 150 years it became usual for the lease to be renewed automatically, so that tenants came to regard the land as their own, which they could sell if they wished. When a sale took place the seller gave the buyer a straw grown on the land, giving rise to the name 'straw tenure', though this transaction was carried out in the presence of an official representative of the Lord which reflected the fact that one tenant was in reality just transferring tenancy of the Lord's land to another individual. By the 17th century this system was well established and recognized by Manx courts and it was confirmed by James I in 1607 when he was Lord. In 1630 Lord Strange sent commissioners to the Island with instructions to discontinue this system and replace it with leases lasting either for three lives or for twenty-one years. They met fierce resistance from the Manx and accomplished very little, but the

James, seventh Earl of Derby. (Courtesy of the Rt Hon. The Earl of Derby 2007)

signal had gone out that Strange was determined to deprive tenants of their ancient 'rights'. This happened in the very decade that Charles I was accused of attempting to do the same in Britain.

In 1629, greatly frustrated by financial and policy restraints imposed upon him by Parliament, Charles I resolved to rule without it and managed to do so for eleven years, building up a dam of discontent year by year. This broke in 1640 when his attempts to interfere with the Presbyterian religion in Scotland provoked a rebellion there, and he called upon his English Parliament to raise money and troops. Instead MPs launched into a determined attempt to prevent him ruling without Parliament again by limiting his royal authority. Charles decided to fight for his rights and raised his standard at Nottingham in August 1642. This put everyone into the dilemma of deciding which side they would support and brother often fought against brother. Some eighty members of the House of Lords supported the king while about fifty sided with Parliament. Strange, despite his opposition to the king's religious policy and the coolness with which he had been treated by Charles, felt bound to support him out of loyalty to his rightful king. He was appointed one of the royalist commanders in the north-west, raising a force of 5,000 men and equipping them at his own expense as well as contributing £40,000 to the king's war chest.

On October 2nd 1642 Strange's father died and he succeeded as the seventh Earl of Derby just as he was besieging a parliamentarian garrison in Manchester. He did not take the town and also failed to prevent Preston and Lancaster falling to the enemy. He made unsuccessful attacks on Bolton and Lancaster in February 1643 and suffered a major defeat at Whalley in April. This poor record led Charles and his advisors to rely less on territorial magnates and more on experienced commanders and James was ordered to defend the Isle of Man, which was thought to be in danger of an attack from Charles' enemies in Scotland, and he arrived on the Island in June 1643.

What he discovered was a strong protest there against his own rule, led by Edward Christian of Maughold and no doubt prompted by the example of the English rebels against a 'tyrannical' king. Christian had spent some time at the Court of Charles I and was a protégé of his favourite the Duke of Buckingham, who had secured for him command of a 34-gun frigate. James met him and was impressed enough to appoint him Governor of the Isle of Man in

1628, a post he held until 1639 when he was dismissed, apparently for becoming too greedy. However, in January 1643 James made use of Christian's military experience by appointing him to train all the able-bodied men in the Island. Christian set up a military camp near the Llhen trench but then proceeded to make his men take an oath of loyalty to him. At the same time, John Greenhalghe, who had been Governor of the Island since 1640, was struggling to deal with strong opposition to the paying of tithes to the Church. One Manxman was committed to prison in May 1643 for refusing to pay but was rescued by a mob, while another cried that he would fight and die first rather than pay. Much of all this was stirred up by Christian, who by now had a good deal of the Island under his control, so Greenalghe announced that he would put the matter before the Earl of Derby himself, and this is how matters stood when James reached the Island in June.

Faced with a perilous situation Derby behaved with Machiavellian skill, being outwardly polite to all though alternately persuading and threatening the Manx as well as sending out informers to mingle with the people and report back to him. He called a meeting of the Lord's Council and the Keys at Peel Castle in July and he had clearly thought carefully about how to deal with troublemakers. He wrote later 'There were some who saucily behaved themselves and of those I put some out of countenance with austere looking on them; troubling their discourse in seeming not to hear well what they said, and asking them to repeat the same; which astonished them so, that oft they did forget the matter they were about, and sometimes feared to speak more of it'. When confronted with eloquent and difficult questioners, however, he sensibly left them to his officials and the deemsters. This meeting agreed to the setting up of a Commission to inquire into grievances and Derby felt able to arrest Edward Christian and several minor troublemakers. Christian was tried in December and it was alleged against him that he had framed a new form of government featuring a House of Keys elected by the people and that he had encouraged opposition to tithes and encouraged mutiny. Moreover he had accused Derby of oppressing the people and showing contempt for Manx law and he had fought for the English Parliament and against Charles I. To judge by this, Edward Christian must be seen as following in the example of John Pym and the English parliamentarians in championing 'democracy' over feudal rule. Christian offered no defence, and he was fined a thousand marks and

111

imprisoned. Lesser offenders were let off more lightly and the rebellion died down.

When he came to the Island in June 1643 Derby had left his wife and children behind the defended walls of Lathom House but in February 1644 it was surrounded by parliamentary troops under Thomas Fairfax, though Lady Derby proved a courageous and inspirational leader of the garrison of 300 men. When he heard about this Derby sailed back to England in March and persuaded the royalist general Prince Rupert to come to the rescue of his home. Rupert won a battle at Stockport on May 25th and marched on to Lathom two days later and ended a siege that had lasted eleven weeks. On the 28th he and Derby recaptured Bolton, though this success was marred by the massacre of a thousand soldiers and civilian men at Rupert's command, with Derby inevitably associated with this misdeed. Rupert and the royalists, including Derby, suffered a heavy defeat at Marston Moor in July 1644, after which the royalists lost control of the North. Lathom was again besieged and Derby sent his wife to the safety of the Isle of Man and joined her there in September. Soon afterwards, Lathom was captured in December and razed to the ground.

Derby and his wife set up home in Castle Rushen, enlarging their residence, Derby House, and attempting to recreate there some of the luxuries and trappings of a small court, with masques, balls and entertainments. Over the years Derby also wrote a number of literary works, including an account of his experiences in the Isle of Man. Meanwhile he set about raising a suitable force in the Island to defend it for the king if necessary and a troop of 72 cavalry was formed, composed of four men from each parish and four officers, with a similar troop set up in 1645. Seven training camps were established, three on the north side and four on the south and by 1649 another two troops of cavalry had been raised, bringing the total to 288. In addition to these the two main castles were garrisoned and there were many English royalist soldiers in the Island. There was also a fort at Douglas on Pollock Rock, built of stone and round in shape, and one on St Michael's Island. Derby also had a small fleet led by a royal frigate and several 16-oared long boats. These raided parliamentarian ships which came too close and in 1644 they got the better of a flotilla of enemy ships on one occasion and beat off an attack on the Calf of Man on another.

Earl James also made use of his enforced residence on the Island to

Castle Rushen, Lord Derby's residence from 1643 to 1651. (Miles Cowsill)

113

make a determined attempt to abolish straw tenure. In 1643 he appointed four commissioners to offer leases of 21 years or three lives to 'straw' tenants and an Act of Tynwald in 1645 declared that selling land without the Lord's permission was illegal, while further regulations confirmed the Lord's right to repossess the land of tenants who were behind with their rent. Many tenants took up the new leases under the impression that they would be free from ancient obligations such as providing food and provisions to the Lord's garrisons and household, but that proved to be a 'grey area' and the whole issue gave rise to increasing discontent. Trade was still insignificant on the Island and Derby rigidly enforced the use of standard measures, which had been introduced as long ago as 1429 but had not generally been observed, and strict punishments were ordained for those who did not possess correct weights and measures. Derby also attempted, with some success, to establish a woollen industry on the Island. He himself wore a suit made of loaghtan wool and he encouraged English craftsmen to come over and set up fulling mills. It crossed his mind to set up a university or college in the Island to 'get friends into the country and enrich this land', as he told his son, but in fact he did nothing to advance this idea.

As part of his drive to raise money and to pay for the expenses of defending the Island Derby decided not to replace Bishop Richard Parr in 1644 and instead carried out the secular responsibilities of the bishop himself, also retaining the episcopal lands and their revenues. These were by no means impressive and indeed the bishopric was not a great prize at this time, its money value being estimated at only £140 in 1635, with rents worth £116 in 1645. Derby might also have decided to hold on to the bishop's lands until the leases expired. Either way, his failure to appoint a bishop, however difficult it might have been to find a suitable candidate given the modest emoluments, is not impressive.

From their safe haven in Castletown the Derbys followed with dismay the collapse of the royalist cause in England. Charles I was decisively defeated at Naseby in June 1645 and in April he surrendered to the Scots at Newark. Dissension then broke out between the three elements among the victors - the Scots, Parliament and the Army - and Charles decided that he could play them off against each other and agreed to Presbyterianism in Scotland in return for Scottish support against Parliament. Oliver Cromwell, who had emerged as leader of a 'New Model Army' which he had trained, crushed the Scots at Preston in August 1648 and insisted that Charles was a traitor and should be tried as such. He expelled from Parliament those who did not agree with this drastic action and Charles was duly tried, found guilty and beheaded outside the Banqueting House in Whitehall on January 30th 1649. Parliament followed this up with an Act abolishing the monarchy and House of Lords and establishing a parliamentary republic which was named 'The Commonwealth'.

During this period Derby made several attempts to save his English lands from being seized by Parliament. After the King's surrender Countess Charlotte travelled to London in 1647 to plead the Derby case, but in vain, and after Charles' execution in 1649 Derby offered to buy back the rights to his estates for a sum of £15,572. This offer was initially accepted and then rejected, and Derby was excluded from amnesties offered to other leading royalists. His continued defence of the Isle of Man was no doubt the main reason for this and in July 1649 he foolishly made an arrogant reply to an official demand from the new Commonwealth that he should surrender the Island, saying that if it troubled him with any more messages, he would burn the paper and hang the bearer. This was dangerously provocative but he was putting his faith in help from Scotland which had been shocked by the execution of Charles I and had immediately proclaimed his nineteen-year-old son king in Scotland as Charles II. Derby announced his allegiance to the new king and invited all royal supporters over to the Isle of Man, from where, he grandly announced, 'we will unanimously employ our forces to the utter ruin of these unmatchable and rebellious regicides, and the final destruction of their interests both by land and sea'. The Commonwealth's response to this fighting talk was formally to dispossess Derby of the lordship of Man in September 1649 and to grant it to General Lord Fairfax, the head of its army. But Fairfax was busy with weightier matters and made no move towards the Island for the moment.

Meanwhile Charles II appointed Derby a knight of the Garter and gave him command of the royalist forces in the north of England in the insurrection which the royalists were planning. During 1650 some of Derby's daughters who were in England were imprisoned and the Government began to sell off his lands. In March 1651 Commonwealth ships at last made an attempt to land troops on the

Island but were beaten off by Derby's naval force. In August Derby appointed his wife as his regent on the Island and sailed for the Lancashire coast with at least seven ships and 300 Manx soldiers, landing on the banks of the river Wyre on the 15th. On the 26th his force was decisively defeated near Wigan and although the Manx soldiers are said to have fought with courage, afterwards, being 'poor naked snakes' they were scattered up and down the country and put to work for English masters, eventually deserting them and making their way home. Derby managed to escape from the battle and he joined Charles II at Worcester where the royal army was crushed by Oliver Cromwell on September 3rd. Charles hid in a tree and Derby helped him to escape to eventual exile abroad for the next nine years. He himself surrendered to Captain Oliver Edge at Newport, in Shropshire, and was imprisoned in Chester Castle.

A court martial tried him for high treason on the grounds that he 'had traitorously borne arms for Charles Stuart against the Parliament; that he was guilty of a breach of an Act of Parliament of the 12th of August, 1651, prohibiting all correspondence with Charles Stuart or any of his party; that he had fortified his house at Lathom against the Parliament; and that he now held the Isle of Man against them'. He was found guilty and condemned to death despite his defence that he had been promised his life when he surrendered to Captain Edge. During his last days he was allowed to see his daughters and also his eldest son Charles, whom he had wrongly suspected of submitting to the Commonwealth. He was then taken to Bolton - where many still associated him with the massacre in 1644 - and beheaded there on October 15th 1651, aged 44.

By tradition he is hailed in the Isle of Man as 'Yn Stanlagh Mooar' - 'The Great Stanley'. It is difficult to see why. He was an unsuccessful commander of royalist forces and made very little impact on the fortunes of the civil war except to be associated with one of its recognized atrocities, at Bolton. On the Isle of Man he nipped in the bud an early attempt to set up an elected House of Keys and caused widespread discontent and eventually revolt by reforming the straw tenure to suit his own interests, and he failed to fill a vacancy in the bishopric in order to increase his own revenues. It could be argued that he was a man of principle and stood loyally by the royalist cause because he believed that it was a just one, but that was an issue more concerned with England than the welfare of the Isle of Man. As we have seen, several of his Stanley predecessors had acted very skilfully

The execution of Lord Derby in Bolton. (Manx National Heritage)

in times of civil war and emerged from the conflicts with enhanced reputations and increased estates. The seventh earl, however, played his cards so badly that he lost everything, including his own life.

THE SAGA OF 'ILLIAM DHONE'

In many ways it is Derby's wife who is more deserving of admiration. Charlotte's spirited defence of Lathom during its long siege caused much comment at the time and one parliamentarian remarked that the countess 'had stolen the earl's breeches when he had fled…into the Isle of Man, and hath in his absence played the man at Lathom'. Other sources suggest that in 1651 it was she who told him that if he did not take action to support Charles II, he had better 'pull off the breeches and she would put them on, and then lead them on'. Not for nothing, evidently, was she a grand-daughter of William the Silent, the hero of the Netherlands, and in the nineteenth century her adventures were romanticized in novels by Sir Walter Scott and others. But her biggest challenge was yet to come because after her husband had set out for England she was forced to deal with a major crisis on the Isle of Man involving William Christian, or 'Illiam Dhone' - brown-haired William - as the Manx called him.

William was a member of the influential Christian family of Milntown and his father Ewan was a deemster and he was also distantly related to Edward Christian, the disgraced Governor. William bought lands near Accrington in Lancashire in 1633 and his father bought the estate of Ronaldsway and handed it over to him in 1643. He was among those named as being members of the Keys in 1637 as well as 1643 and he was appointed water-bailiff (chief customs officer) by Derby in 1644. Four years later he became receiver-general, responsible for collecting the lord's rents and customs duties. This was all at the time when Derby, as we have seen, was attempting to increase his revenues from the Island and seeking to abolish the straw tenure. Christian himself accepted a lease of three lives on his Ronaldsway property in 1643.

So when Derby left the Island in August 1651 William Christian was well-connected, a significant landowner and a long-standing servant of the Derby regime. He was not the Governor of the Island, a post held by the experienced and trusted John Greenhalghe who died at a critical moment in September and was replaced by Sir Philip Musgrave. In the same month news arrived of the collapse of the royalist cause at Worcester and it became clear to all those in positions of authority in the Island that further attempts to hold out against the Commonwealth would in the end be futile. Even Lady Derby came to this conclusion and without consulting any of the Manx authorities she sent a letter to Beaumaris addressed to Colonel Robert Duckenfield, who had been appointed by the Commonwealth to lead an expedition to capture the Island, effectively offering to surrender it in return for the life of her husband. William Christian got to know about this and feared that a surrender of this kind would be a grave risk to the ancient rights and liberties of the Island. After all, the Commonwealth had already abolished the monarchy and the House of Lords in England: why should it care about any constitutional claims of the Isle of Man when it would be much more advantageous to incorporate it into one of the north-western counties?

Accordingly 800 men assembled at Christian's house at Ronaldsway on October 19th and took an oath that they would not recognize any action of Lady Derby until she agreed to support their demands - which were that the Island's ancient rights and customs should be recognized after any surrender, and in particular the straw tenure. Christian's men then took control of all the Island's forts, though the two major castles remained under forces loyal to the Countess. When Duckenfield's ships arrived off Ramsey on October

25th, Christian sent a message out to them saying that there would be no opposition to the landing of his troops, showing that his aim was probably to come to a separate agreement with the invaders. Duckenfield's men moved into siege positions outside Peel Castle and Castle Rushen and on October 29th he sent a message to the Countess inside Castle Rushen asking her to come to terms and referring to her husband as 'the late' Earl of Derby, which was the first she knew of his execution.

Lady Derby was stunned by this, it seems, and was not able to gather her thoughts towards making acceptable proposals. Then she was betrayed by soldiers within the castle who opened a sally-port on October 31st and let the besiegers into the outer wall and tower. After this Charlotte gave in and agreed to surrender both castles in return for being permitted to leave the Island with her family and friends, as a result of which she was hailed by royalists as being the

Charlotte, Countess of Derby. (Manx National Heritage)

William Christian, 'Illiam Dhone'. (Manx National Heritage)

last individual to surrender property to the Commonwealth. Her position was undoubtedly undermined by the actions of William Christian and by the disloyalty of her own garrison and if she had enjoyed the full support of the Manx people it is likely that the very formidable defences of Castle Rushen could have held out for a long time. On the other hand, the rules of warfare in those days permitted severe punishment for a garrison which insisted on holding out when there was realistically no hope of success, and this was probably a case when, for the good of the Manx people and the future of the Island, discretion - some would call it treason - was the better part of valour.

Duckenfield's agreement with Charlotte was approved in November and Parliament passed an Act stating that the Island should 'be taken in as part of England, yet retaining such laws already established as are equitable and just and more suitable to the people than any other that can be imposed'. Given that the Commonwealth had already granted the Lordship to Lord Fairfax in 1649 this effectively meant that it permitted the Island to remain under a 'monarchical' form of government and did not envisage any radical change in its status or laws. Fairfax was formally proclaimed Lord in Castletown in February 1652 in the presence of the 24 Keys and four men from each parish, though he did not attend in person.

Fairfax was one of the most distinguished and honourable of the major figures involved in the English Civil War. Born the eldest son of the second Lord Fairfax at the family home near Otley in Yorkshire in 1612 he became a professional soldier before he was twenty and played a significant part in Charles I's campaigns against the Scots from 1639 onwards, receiving a knighthood for his services in 1641. However, when the King raised his standard in 1642 Fairfax followed his father in supporting Parliament and played a leading role in the royalist defeat at Marston Moor. Early in 1645 Parliament elected him Lord General of the New Model Army because of his military reputation and also the respect in which he was held by the 'Puritans' for his godly beliefs and behaviour. He defeated the royalists at Naseby in June and took Bristol in September, where he was praised for his clemency and the discipline of his troops. He then received the surrender of the royalist capital at Oxford in 1646, which ended the first civil war. Under Fairfax the New Model Army did not lose a single battle, siege or storm. But he was a soldier, not a politician, and he had no taste for the politicking and manoeuvering which followed.

In 1648 he succeeded his father as the third Lord Fairfax and led

Lord Fairfax. (Manx National Heritage)

the army when fighting resumed again, becoming involved in a long siege of Colchester after which he executed the royalist commanders and uncharacteristically permitted stern punishment for the defenders. During this year the main influence in the army was Fairfax' second-in-command, Oliver Cromwell, supported by Henry Ireton, and it was they who pressed for the execution of the king, which Fairfax resisted to the point of not signing the death warrant. Finally, in 1650 he resigned as Lord General when Parliament instructed him to invade Scotland in a pre-emptive strike against Charles II, arguing that he would defend England to the death but that he would not invade the Scots, his former allies. He was replaced as Lord General by Oliver Cromwell and retired to his home at Nunappleton Hall in Yorkshire where he lived quietly, involved in literary pursuits and his religious devotions.

This period of inactivity should have given Fairfax the opportunity to take an interest in his role as Lord of Man but he never visited the Island, possibly because he had been wounded many times in his campaigns and suffered chronic ill-health, especially from gout. All the same, it is surprising that someone with an active and adventurous record such as his was not curious to see his Island 'kingdom'. However, as a true Yorkshireman he was interested to know how much it was worth to him and he appointed commissioners to establish the number of tenants and the value of their rents. Colonel Duckenfield served as his Governor in 1651 and was replaced by Matthew Cadwell the following year and William Christian ('Illiam Dhone') in 1656. Christian also continued to serve

A statue of Colonel Robert Duckenfield, arguably a conqueror of the Isle of Man, recently erected in his home town of Dukinfield, near Manchester. (Tameside Council)

123

as receiver-general, responsible for all the lord's revenues and also those of the diocese (there was still no bishop) and the former monastic lands.

Christian was Governor for two years and was replaced in 1659 by James Chaloner, an experienced lawyer and former English judge, who had been deputy-governor for some years. He was also the author of 'A Short Treatise of the Isle of Man', published in 1656, one of the earliest accounts of the Island's history. Fairfax instructed him to undertake a comprehensive audit of the Island's financial affairs and in 1659 Chaloner took the explosive step of removing Christian from the office of receiver-general on the grounds that his accounts for the years 1650-1659 were full of irregularities and suggested that he had embezzled about £1,000. Under this pressure, Christian left the Island and lived on his lands in Lancashire, though on the Island his son George seems to have produced accounts which exonerated his father.

By 1660 events in England had taken a dramatic turn following the death of Oliver Cromwell in 1658. The enthusiastic radicals who had set up the Commonwealth in 1650 had come to realize through bitter experience that it was not an easy thing to write a paper constitution and make it work smoothly. The first Commonwealth parliament had proved to be corrupt and self-seeking, and it was (illegally) dismissed by Oliver Cromwell and his soldiers who replaced it with an appointed assembly of 'good' men, known for their piety. They proved to be hopelessly inexperienced and incompetent, so Cromwell himself reluctantly became 'Lord Protector' and ruled with a Council and a one-chamber parliament. He was a king in all but name but he refused to accept the crown, though he appointed his eldest son Richard as his successor. Richard had no stomach for the job and resigned in 1659 after which there was confusion and civil war loomed again, with General Lambert making a bid to become Lord Protector. This had its ramifications on the Island because Lieutenant Hathorne, the officer in charge of Peel Castle, acted upon orders from Lambert's supporters and arrested Governor Chaloner, imprisoning him at Peel on November 22nd

Another civil war was prevented by the resolute action of two strong military men: one was General George Monck, who was in charge of Scotland, and the other was Lord Fairfax who came out of retirement to join Monck in declaring themselves in favour of the restoration of King Charles II. Their influence proved decisive, especially as many ordinary people in England were disillusioned with the arbitrary and unstable regimes which had followed one another during the past decade. It was agreed that the clock should be put back to 1642 and the king should rule with a House of Commons and House of Lords as before. Charles made vague promises to respect Parliament's wishes and not to take revenge and he was welcomed into London by rejoicing crowds in 1660. Meanwhile on the Island Chaloner was released and in May Charles II was proclaimed king with shouting, shooting of muskets and ordnance, the drinking of beer and great rejoicing. Unfortunately Chaloner died soon afterwards as a result of ill-health contracted during his weeks in Peel Castle.

General Monck was lavishly rewarded for his part in Charles' restoration with a dukedom and estates but Fairfax, as ever uninterested in politics, was content to withdraw again into retirement in Yorkshire. One of the main principles of the 'Restoration Settlement' was that royalists whose lands had been confiscated should receive them back and this meant that Fairfax relinquished the Lordship of Man, which reverted to Charles, the eighth Earl of Derby, who also recovered most of his Stanley inheritance in England. Fairfax provided the horse that Charles II used at his coronation and then lived quietly until his death in 1671.

Among those who had gone to London for a sight of the new king was William Christian, but while there he was arrested for a debt of £20,000 and spent nearly a year in the Fleet prison, though it is not clear whether or not this debt was related to his affairs in the Isle of Man. Meanwhile Parliament passed an Act of Indemnity which granted a pardon to all except named regicides and apparently having been advised that this applied to the Isle of Man Christian returned home in September 1662. Arguing that Lord Justice Coke had ruled decades before that the Island was not a part of the kingdom of England and that an Act of Parliament did not apply to it unless the Island was specifically mentioned, Earl Charles issued a warrant for Christian's arrest and trial 'for all his illegal actions and rebellions' in 1651.

In November 1662 a six-man jury on the Island indicted him for treason but at his trial in the court of general gaol delivery Christian refused to plead. The deputy governor, Henry Nowell, then consulted Deemster Norris about what should be done in this case and Norris consulted the Keys whose majority opinion was that

Christian should be judged to be at the mercy of the Lord of Man for his life and goods. Because he wanted a unanimous opinion seven members of the Keys were dismissed on Derby's orders and replaced by more amenable men who unanimously authorized the death sentence. Nowell ordered that Christian should not suffer the normal traitor's fate of being hanged, drawn and quartered, but he was shot by a firing squad on January 2nd 1663, on Hango Hill outside Castletown, using his last moments to make an eloquent and patriotic speech and to die with courage.

Christian had sent a petition to Charles II and the Privy Council arguing that Derby's action was a violation of the Act of Indemnity but this did not reach London until a week after his death. In due course the Privy Council called before them Derby, the deemsters and three of those who had tried Christian and pronounced that 'the Act of General Pardon and Indemnity did and ought to be understood to extend to the Isle of Man'. Christian's estates were to be restored to his heirs and as expiation for his unjust death, the deemsters were detained in prison for a time. Three other participants in the 1651 rebellion who had been imprisoned by Derby without trial were ordered to be released and compensated for their ordeal.

Views vary as to whether Christian was a 'martyr' or a 'traitor' and the arguments will probably continue, partly because we are never likely to be sure of all the facts. His decision to abandon Countess Charlotte was certainly disloyal but probably wise politically and as to whether he should have suffered a traitor's death, there is the heavyweight legal decision of the Privy Council that he should not. On the separate and lesser issue of whether he embezzled money entrusted to his care - of which there were persistent allegations - we have little proof now except that he was thought worthy of nearly a year in the Fleet prison for debt. We are told by a historian of the Stanleys that Earl Charles was a person 'of great affability, a kind landlord, and a loving friend and neighbour', but he comes very badly out of the William Christian affair. Against the whole spirit of the Restoration Settlement, through which he had received back his own estates, he pursued a vindictive campaign against Christian, even to the point of packing juries with his own supporters. Moreover his interpretation of the law was declared false by the Privy Council which means that in legal terms, at least, he had the blood of Christian on his hands.

Chapter Ten
The Last Stanleys,
1660-1736

EARL CHARLES, 1660-1672

During the sixteenth and seventeenth centuries the most obvious physical development on the Island was the growth of the main towns of Castletown, Peel, Ramsey and Douglas and the building of a number of larger houses in the countryside for the main landowners. Castletown was the chief seat of the Lord, his Governors and the law courts and during the residence there of the seventh earl in the 1640s it grew considerably and had one formal street and a handsome market place with a cross in the middle. However, in the succeeding years it failed to develop into a large town. Peel had a good harbour but it remained a relatively small fishing port, while Ramsey was even smaller. By 1681 Douglas had outstripped everywhere else and it was described then as 'the place of the greatest resort in the whole Island, because the haven is commodious ...unto which the Frenchmen and other foreigners are use to repair'. By 1690 the customs duties (to the nearest pound) paid by Castletown were £7, by Ramsey £13, by Peel £16 and by Douglas £31, which gives an indication of their relative importance. Ramsey's growth had suffered a setback in about 1630 when most of its houses had been swept away by the sea during a violent storm.

William Blundell, a Lancashire gentleman who lived in the Island between 1648 and 1660, wrote an account of the Island during this time and commented that in the towns three quarters of the inhabitants were Manxmen and a quarter 'foreigners'. In the towns there was a growing number of shopkeepers who were among the most prosperous citizens, often owning two or three properties. Of the Manx in general Blundell reckoned that they were mostly mariners and fishermen who, though not rich, lived well enough. The homes of country folk he described as being 'mere hovels, compacted of stones and clay for the walls, thatched with broom, most commonly having one room only' and in time-honoured fashion animals still lodged indoors with the family. This contrasted with the upper classes on the Island, whose lifestyle Blundell compared to the

127

Charles, eighth Earl of Derby. (Manx National Heritage)

gentry of his native Lancashire, describing Manx gentry houses as high, handsome and well-built. By now these people were all speaking good English, compared with the lower classes, who spoke Manx Gaelic. Based on the number of tenants on the manorial rolls, the population of the Island in 1660 was probably about 12,000, only a small proportion of whom lived in the towns.

Having resumed control over his father's lordship of Man in 1660 Earl Charles did not follow his policy with regard to the Church because one of his first actions was to set up a commission to 'restore the collapsed and most deplorable estate and condition of religion and the Church as well'. In 1661 he filled the long-vacant see by appointing Archdeacon Samuel Rutter as bishop, followed by Isaac

Barrow in 1663. Barrow, who could speak no Manx, was not impressed with his new diocese, writing that he found the people 'loose and vicious in their lives, rude and barbarous in their behaviour, and…without any true sense of religion.….Their ministers, it is true, took upon them to preach but were themselves much fitter to be taught, being very ignorant and wholly illiterate, having had no education than what that rude place afforded them.' He deplored the fact that there were very few books on the Island and that the clergy lived in poverty, having to supplement their incomes by keeping ale-houses. Barrow persuaded Earl Charles to grant his right to the Church tithes on a 10,000 year lease to an 'Impropriate Fund', which would assist poor clergy and church schools, in return for £1,000 which Barrow raised on his own initiative in England. In 1664 Barrow was appointed Governor in addition to being bishop and from this position of power he managed to acquire two farms at Hango Hill and Ballagilley, effectively confiscating them from their tenant, John Lace, who claimed to hold them by straw tenure. It was Barrow's intention to establish a school there with this endowment but his aim was not achieved until King William's College was founded much later, in 1833.

Barrow's high-handed treatment of Lace reflected Earl Charles' lack of respect for the constitutional position of the Keys. Between 1430 and 1580 it seems that no new laws were passed and the Keys, as we have seen, were generally nominated by the Lord or his officials from time to time to give advice as needed. From about 1600 the appearance of the same names in the Statute Book suggests that the Keys were increasingly chosen from a recognized pool of individuals and in 1659, during the governorship of James Chaloner, the deemsters declared that 'When any of the 24 Keys die, or are removed, the rest of the number shall recommend some fit persons to supply their places and shall give their names either to the Lord or the Governor'. As to their function at this time Chaloner himself stated that their assistance was only called for by the Governor and officers 'in cases of doubt and considerations… about the ordering of the affairs of the country, for the defence and safety thereof; and propositions of good and wholesome laws and orders for the peace and welfare of the people in matters of right betwixt the Lord and the people, and betwixt party and party'.

Earl Charles clearly considered that he had the right to remove from office members of the Keys who did not follow his instructions because, as we have seen, he replaced seven members during the trial of William Christian in 1662 and he was very heavy-handed over the repercussions of the Lace affair. Like his father he was anxious to do away with the straw tenure and had therefore encouraged Barrow to dispossess Lace of his two farms near Castletown in 1664. Burning with a sense of injustice, Lace appealed to the Keys in 1666 and they concluded - being landowners themselves - that he had a right to the land, or at least to compensation for losing it. They then ignored a warning from Derby that this action greatly displeased him and he announced that

> Having too great an evidence of the unquiet and factious humour that rules in several of my 24 Keys...and finding they endeavour to establish a right to their farms in themselves not only to the overthrow of my just dues and prerogatives in the Island, while they challenge an unlimited title to their own tenements beyond the term of their leases ...it is my will and command to all my officers that the estates of the foresaid persons be at the expiration of their leases seized upon for my use and none of them be admitted to compound for their estates without special licence obtained under my hand ...and I also require that the foresaid persons shall be put out of all places of office and command in the Island.

This broadside had the desired effect and the Keys gave their written assent to the grant of Lace's land to Bishop Barrow.

EARLS WILLIAM AND JAMES, 1672-1736

Earl Charles died in 1672 and he was succeeded by his son William, the ninth earl, who was about seventeen, and until he reached his majority in 1676 the Island's affairs were supervised first by his mother and then by the Duke of Ormonde. In 1673 Tynwald was prevailed upon to confirm that no land should be disposed of without the Lord's permission and increasingly tenants became discouraged from farming land because of the insecurity of their position. Earl William visited the Island in 1686 and presided over Tynwald at St John's in 1691. Two years later he appointed commissioners to manage the Island's revenue and to let all land then out of lease, of which there was a good deal. The commissioners found it so difficult to attract tenants that William came to the Island himself in 1699 and announced that he intended to solve this issue to the general satisfaction, and he asked Bishop Thomas Wilson to look into the problem and make some suitable proposals. He was clearly well acquainted with the Island and interested in its welfare because in 1698 he made some notes about all the things that needed to be done:

> Continue the linen manufacture. The lighthouse and a good smithy in it. The soap boiling. The Pottery. Set up a brewhouse and malthouse. Perfect Derby Haven. Search for mines. Open the road to Peel, etc. Improve the maintenance of the clergy. Repair the church and castle at Peel. Get a good woollen clothier, a good tanner and curier. Form a register. If possible form a company for trade. Improve the husbandries. An Act for the education of youths. Reform the ale houses. But above all settle the property of the people. Put the laws into writing and reduce the practical part to method. Apply one of the academic places to the service of the state that one be always educated in the Comptroller's office to breed Attorney-Generals, Deemsters, etc.

Before any further action could be taken over the land question Earl William died in 1702 in his late forties and he was succeeded by his younger brother James, the tenth earl. He was a professional soldier who served in an English regiment in the Netherlands where he had come to the favourable notice of William of Orange. In 1688 William, backed in England by Protestant opponents of the unpopular Catholic King James II, invaded the country and he and his wife Mary (the daughter of James II) were proclaimed joint King and Queen by Parliament and James was forced into exile. This 'Glorious Revolution' significantly increased the authority of Parliament which had effectively deposed one king and replaced him with another, a serious blow to the Stuart notion of the 'divine right' of kings. James Stanley fought with distinction in Flanders and Ireland and held an appointment at William's court. When he succeeded his brother there were a number of law suits to be settled with his niece Lady Ashburnham, who claimed a considerable share of her father's estates, and these were not resolved until 1715. In 1703 James fought with Marlborough in the Netherlands and was promoted major-general though he resigned his commission in 1705 on his marriage to Mary Morley, a rich heiress. He lived with his new wife at Knowsley which he considerably enlarged and decorated with a fine collection of Italian paintings but sadly their only child, a son, died in infancy, a loss that would eventually have considerable repercussions within the Stanley family and on the Isle of Man.

Soon after his succession Earl James showed his awareness of the seriousness of the continuing land dispute by informing Bishop Thomas Wilson that 'the sooner the Island can be settled on a good bottom it will be much better for both the Island and myself'. Wilson and three members of the Keys travelled to Knowsley to meet him and presented their proposals for resolving the issue, most of which he accepted. In June 1704 a Land Settlement Act was promulgated at Tynwald, described by some commentators as the 'Manx Magna Carta'. In the Act the Lord declared and confirmed to his tenants 'their ancient customary estates of inheritance in their respective tenements, descendable from ancestor to heir according to the laws and customs of the Isle', while tenants were obliged to pay the fees for their tenancies fixed in 1643. This was, of course, a 'victory' for those who had resisted the policies of the seventh earl and his successors in attempting to do away with the 'straw tenure'. By the Act the tenants, who now paid a fixed Lord's rent, became in reality the owners of their land, with rights of inheritance and sale. A good many further detailed clauses were included in the Act, which was confirmed in 1777 and remained the basis of the tenure of most Manx estates well into the 20th century.

Earl James' decision to bring an end to the long-running and damaging land dispute was entirely sensible though he eventually came to regret the loss of revenue to him that the agreement entailed. He also had to face a situation where the Keys were attempting to flex their muscles in a more general sense. The English Parliament's constitutional victory in 1688 is likely to have encouraged the Keys to press for further recognition of their own status. Governor William Sacheverell (1693-96) regarded them as the 'representatives of the country' who 'in conjunction with the Governor and officers make the legislative power of the nation' and other authorities noted that 'no new law can be made, or custom introduced or abolished' without the consent of the Keys and the deemsters. But in 1697 the Keys complained to Earl William about what they considered the arbitrary action of the Governor, Colonel Nicholas Sankey, who had in their view overstepped his authority, ignored their constitutional role and even committed two members of the Keys to prison for objecting to his policies. Earl William responded by granting the Keys a commission to inquire into any irregularities committed by the Governor and his officers. Soon after his succession, Earl James was asked by the Keys to agree to legislation which would expressly require the consent of the Keys to matters of public concern and the imposition of customs duties, but he took no action.

In 1715 the Keys objected to being treated by the Governor as if they were an ordinary criminal jury but he replied that if they did not give a verdict in writing on a recent case, they would be imprisoned. When they did not satisfy his requirements, he did indeed imprison them in Castle Rushen and fined them 20 shillings each into the bargain. In 1719 John Stevenson, a member of the Keys, went to Knowsley and presented a petition to Derby and some members of his Council who were also there, complaining of this kind of 'illegal' punishment of the Keys and also accusing the Governor's officers of lining their own pockets from fees and customs dues. Along with the petition went a threat that if Derby did nothing about these complaints, the Keys would go over his head to the Crown. In response to this Derby made a number of conciliatory promises but none of them were kept because the Governor's Council subsequently refused to agree to proposals which would have redressed the grievances of the Keys. Moreover, they tried John Stevenson for criminal activity and in 1723 censured the Keys for supporting him. After this the Keys made their threatened appeal to the Crown and Derby was told in 1725 that 'the affair of the Island has been mentioned to Sir Robert Walpole and next Tuesday they meet to fix on the heads of what concession your Lordship is to make'.

The petition of the Keys was passed from the Crown to Derby who instructed the Governor and Council to prepare a report for the Privy Council. This said that the Land Settlement Act of 1704 had been a great benefit to the Island but since then the Manx people had been acting too independently, egged on by the Keys whose claim to be the representatives of the people the report rejected on the grounds that they had long been 'called together and dismissed, placed and displaced by the Lord of the Isle or his Lieutenant as they saw cause.' In fact the report never went before the Privy Council and Governor Horton took revenge by dismissing eleven of the Keys and replacing them with his own nominees. Drastic action of this sort must have had the tacit approval of Derby, who in affairs concerning the Island's government took a distinctly reactionary line despite his record in England of supporting the 'Glorious Revolution' of 1688. He also supported the Hanoverian Succession of 1713 when again the English Parliament excluded the Catholic Stuarts from the throne in favour of the nearest Protestant heir, George, the ruler of the German principality of Hanover. Under the Whig-dominated Hanoverian regime Britain made important strides forward towards parliamentary democracy, but on the Isle of Man the Governors of the tenth Earl of Derby ruled with a despotic touch.

CHURCH AND STATE 1660-1736

Isaac Barrow had been both Bishop and Governor, so during his episcopate (1663-1671), church and state walked in step. A High Anglican and follower of the late Archbishop Laud he did a great deal to lay the foundations for improved educational facilities in the Island and insisted on the strict observance of the Anglican religion as well as high moral standards. But the stipend of the bishop was very modest (about £300 by now) and in 1669 he became Bishop of St Asaph as well. When he resigned the Manx bishopric in 1671 he was replaced by Henry Bridgman (1671-1682) who made only two visits to the Island during his tenure, and then by John Lake (1682-1684) who visited it once. Baptist Levinz, bishop from 1684 to 1693, complained about the Island being 'a poor desolate place' and his title of bishop being too big for his 'scant fortunes to maintain'. However, he was pleased to report to the Archbishop of Canterbury that 'God be thanked, I find the people in appearance nothing inclined to popery'. His most useful contribution to Island life was probably the establishment in 1689 of a school in Peel funded from a bequest made in 1652 by Philip Christian, a member of the Clothworkers Company. When Levinz died in 1693 the bishopric was left vacant, as was the parish of Rushen, in order that the emoluments could be used to repair St German's cathedral. This had been seriously neglected between 1644 and 1661, when there were no bishops, and when the short-lived Bishop Rutter died in 1662 we are told that he was buried 'under the uncovered steeple of St German's, then in ruins'. Between 1693 and 1698 it was provided with a new roof covered with blue slate and general repairs were carried out, though the tower was still left open to the sky.

The bishop appointed in 1698 was one of the Isle of Man's most remarkable figures, Thomas Wilson. Born the son of a Cheshire farmer in 1663 he attended Trinity College Dublin and served as a priest in the diocese of Kildare in Ireland. In 1692 he became tutor to Earl William's family and in 1697 William appointed him bishop in the Isle of Man at the unusually early age of 34. As we have seen William called upon Wilson to draw up proposals for the resolution of the land dispute which Earl James largely accepted in 1704. Also in 1704 Wilson produced his 'Ecclesiastical Constitutions' in which he set out to impose strict observance of Anglican morals and religious practice on the Island at a time when, after the scandalous loose-living of the Restoration, the Anglican Church in England generally entered upon a slack and corrupt era which lasted for much of the eighteenth century - an age of 'Enlightenment' when intellectuals questioned many features of religious belief.

The main offences usually dealt with by the Church Courts were failure to observe saints' days, immorality of various kinds, drunkenness and swearing. In Wilson's first 28 years the same number of cases were brought before the courts as in the previous 38, though the punishments were generally less severe. The law permitted corporal punishment and the barbarous practice of being towed behind a boat in the sea which was meted out to an adulteress, Catherine Kinraid, and is often quoted to the bishop's discredit. Wilson did reduce the fines imposed by the ecclesiastical courts and as these went to the Lord's treasury Governors from about 1713 began to question his right to do this. In 1716 a conflict took place when Wilson excommunicated a woman who had refused to do penance for an offence. She appealed to Derby, who summoned Wilson to a hearing of the case. He refused to attend and was initially fined £10, though this was remitted eventually. Wilson carried on with the rigorous imposition of discipline because, as he put it, 'not only evil practices but evil books and evil notions are becoming very common'.

In 1720 Governor Alexander Horne refused to supply a soldier to convey church offenders to prison and in 1721 he fined and imprisoned the bishop's registrar and summoned Wilson and his vicars-general to answer three charges, which were 'First, that the Ecclesiastical Court assume to themselves a power of hearing and

Bishop Thomas Wilson. (Manx National Heritage)

determining causes in their Court contrary to the rules that the statute law of this Isle directs.....Secondly that the Lord Bishop of this Isle calls a convocation .....at times and for causes that are not comprehended in the law for calling a convocation .....Thirdly, that the said Court have taken upon them to summon persons not within their jurisdiction, contrary to the known laws of this Isle'. Wilson refused to answer the summons and for a time the issue lapsed. In 1722 a petty row involving slanderous remarks made by the Governor's wife about another woman escalated until Wilson suspended his Archdeacon, Horrobin, for supporting Mrs Horne against his own judgement. As the Archdeacon was also the Governor's chaplain, Horne argued that Wilson had no authority over him and without the consent of the Keys fined the bishop £50 and his vicars-general £20 each. They all refused to pay the fines and were accordingly imprisoned in Castle Rushen in June 1722, cut off from letters and friends and treated with considerable harshness.

This deplorable state of affairs lasted for nine weeks, during which time the prisoners appealed to the Privy Council, which eventually ordered their release. In 1724 the Privy Council ruled that the Governor's judgement and fines were illegal and Alexander Horne's arrest was authorized but he had resigned in 1723 and seems to have escaped punishment. Derby was not prepared to accept defeat and in 1725 he appointed Thomas Horton as Governor and gave him authority to declare that the Island's spiritual laws had been abolished when it became part of the province of York in 1542 and he subsequently refused to consider a review of the laws by the Keys. Again Wilson appealed to the Privy Council but this time nothing was done to support his position and between 1725 and 1736, faced with the hostility of Lord Derby and Governor Horton, Wilson's campaign to increase the authority of the Church Courts began to crumble.

THE RISE OF 'SMUGGLING', 1660-1736

Given that the Privy Council was bombarded from 1724 with appeals to it from the House of Keys and from Bishop Wilson regarding the alleged misgovernment of Lord Derby and his officials, it is not surprising that the wily Sir Robert Walpole, generally considered the first UK 'Prime Minister', was beginning to think in terms of putting an end to the rule of the House of Stanley in the Isle of Man. It was not the internal Manx constitutional or ecclesiastical wrangles that really worried the British Government, however, but the problem of the Island's increasingly crucial role as a centre of what the UK considered to be 'smuggling' on a grand scale.

Until about 1660 most Manx people made their living by fishing or agriculture and participation in trade was not extensive or very lucrative and consisted mainly of exporting the Island's excess produce to Britain in return for basic necessities. Over the next few decades, however, the Manx found themselves in the middle of a golden pond because tobacco and tea became very fashionable and popular in Britain and the Crown decided to cash in on this situation by imposing very high import duties on them. They also charged high duties on wines and spirits from 'enemy' countries such as France in the hope that this would injure their economies. On the Isle of Man duties were payable to the Lord but only at a low rate and it soon became clear that if Manxmen could buy tobacco, tea, brandy, spirits and wines in countries such as France, Spain, Portugal, Norway and Sweden, convey them to Douglas, pay the low duty set by Lord Derby and then have them taken in small boats to conveniently quiet locations on the north-west coast of Britain, they could sell them at a very considerable profit to illegal British dealers. Just at this time square-rigged ships were giving way to a new design of smaller boats with fore-and-aft sails which were able to navigate creeks and bays more easily and of course the Manx were seafarers to their fingertips.

In 1671 Britain set up a new Customs Board and in 1672 passed the Navigation Act which said that goods could only be brought into Britain in British ships. Shortly after this Britain attempted to establish customs officers on the Island which inevitably led to protests from the Stanleys, who argued that it was an intrusion into their jurisdiction. Nevertheless British customs men maintained a presence on the Island and were able to report back on the growing volume of illegal trade. When William III went to war with France in 1689 the customs duties on French goods were increased yet again, as were duties on salt and all East India and China goods, and this made smuggling even more worthwhile. In 1707 the Act of Union with Scotland resulted in the establishment of a Customs Board in Edinburgh charged with imposing the same tariffs that were operating in England and this served to make the Government in London even more aware of how much potential revenue they were losing as a result of Manx smugglers. As early as 1711 Earl James was hearing rumours that he was to be offered £50,000 for the Island, which of course he considered a derisory sum. To ward off such an event, Tynwald in the same year passed an Act prohibiting the shipping of foreign goods from the Island to Britain as long as Britain permitted Manx produce to enter Britain duty free. Britain did not make this concession, however, and Tynwald accordingly suspended the 1711 Act and the smuggling went on, by which time the UK duty on tea, for instance, had reached the enormous level of five shillings per pound.

In 1720 Manx smuggling entered a new phase when Earl James farmed out the right to collect his Manx customs duties to two merchants, Josiah Poole from Liverpool and Richard Maguire from Dublin. He charged them a thousand guineas a year, but they ensured a good return on that investment by also running a very profitable smuggling business. This came to the notice of Sir Robert Walpole who offered to buy them out but on being rejected he initiated legislation resulting in an Act of 1726 which prohibited the importation to Britain of any goods whatever from the Isle of Man unless they were Manx produce. This Act also contained a very threatening clause which empowered the Treasury to consider purchasing what it described as 'Lord Derby's dominion of Man'. Alarmed by this development Derby withdrew the customs farm from Poole and Maguire but there were plenty of others to take their places, albeit less prominently, and the smuggling continued as before.

One of the most damaging effects of smuggling internally was that the Island became increasingly awash with alcohol and the comparatively mild 'jough' or traditional beer was replaced first with relatively inexpensive wines and then with spirits. The earliest record of a licence to sell liquor is in 1637 but by the end of the century ale-houses were very numerous and in 1714 it was recorded that 'many of the people are of late become not only tipplers, but also infamous for sottishness and drunkenness'. An Act of Tynwald limited the number of ale-houses to 200 in 1734, but this was increased to 300 only ten years later.

THE LAST STANLEY LORD, 1736.

Earl James died at Knowsley in February 1736, aged 71, leaving no surviving children. He had himself succeeded his brother, who left no sons, and despite the fact that their father, Earl Charles, had reared fifteen children there was a crisis in the House of Stanley because the earldom could only descend through the male line and the nearest male heir was a very distant cousin, Edward Stanley, whom genealogists had to trace by going back in the family tree over 200 years and then back down again. He became the eleventh earl and received some of the Stanley estates but not the Isle of Man because James I's grant of 1609 to the sixth earl stipulated that the Island should pass to the heirs of his eldest son (later the seventh earl), through the female line if necessary. After the execution of the seventh earl in 1651 his widow Countess Charlotte had devoted much of her time to arranging advantageous marriages for her three daughters, who might otherwise have been placed in straitened circumstances. Her third daughter Amelia was duly married in 1659 to John Murray, later Marquess of Atholl, and in 1736 the Isle of Man passed to their grandson James Murray, the second Duke of Atholl, and 330 years of Stanley lordship came to an end.

It could reasonably be argued that throughout this period the rule of the Stanleys had not been distinguished and that successive Lords in the main showed very little personal interest in the Island and felt no strong obligation to improve its infrastructure and economy or attend to the welfare of its people. Given that the lordship was an almost autonomous principality not unlike many of the small states that emerged in Italy and Germany during the same period, where the ruling houses often put a great deal of effort and imagination into the administration of their patrimonies, the potential for development of the Isle of Man during the Stanley period was very considerable. However, the Stanleys were generally content to leave the Island in the hands of their officials, whose main task was to make sure that income exceeded expenditure so that possession of the Island was not actually a financial liability. In 1511 the income from rents alone was £700 and £1,430 in 1609, with the expenses of government only about £300, so the Stanleys were making a profit, if not a large one. When Earl James died in 1736 his surplus revenue was in the region of £1,500 and showing signs of rising sharply because of the profits of the 'running trade'. By 1746 surplus revenue had reached £2,850, by 1752, £4,250 and by 1763, £7,300.

Ownership of the Island and the quasi-regal status that went with it was a matter of significant prestige and it was also important strategically. For this reason it was probably necessary that rich and powerful noblemen such as the Earls of Derby should have assumed responsibility for the Island, but the disadvantage of this was that their main interest and concerns were concentrated on affairs in England, so that to them the Island was inevitably a side-show. If the Lords had been men with less stature and fewer interests in England, they might well have concentrated more on developing their main asset, the Isle of Man. On the other hand less high-profile Lords might not have been able to protect the Island from outside interference as successfully as the powerful Stanleys managed to do. One thing is clear, however. The Stanleys lost the Island just at the moment when as a result of 'the running trade' it was developing into a major financial asset.

Chapter Eleven
The Island and the
Dukes of Atholl, 1736-1830

THE ATHOLL LORDSHIP, 1736-1765

The Murrays of Tullibardine were a long-established Scottish aristocratic family who were granted the earldom of Atholl in 1629 and the marquessate in 1676 and most of the family estates were in Perthshire, centred on the historic Blair Castle. Amelia Stanley's son the second marquess served Queen Anne as Lord Privy Seal and was created a duke in 1703. His eldest son joined the Jacobite rebellion in 1715 which unsuccessfully opposed the succession to the throne of George I and he was attainted by Parliament for high treason. This put the family under a cloud and when the first duke died in 1724 all the rights of inheritance of his eldest son were transferred by Act of Parliament to his second son, James, who accordingly became the second duke in 1724 and Lord of Man in 1736.

He inherited an Island which the tenth Earl of Derby had governed badly, provoking major constitutional conflicts with the House of Keys and a long-running dispute with the much-admired Bishop Wilson. Derby had also turned a blind eye to much of the smuggling activity, which was beneficial to his own finances but which so provoked the British Government that in 1726 it had formulated plans to terminate the Stanley lordship in order to assume responsibity for the customs and to stamp out smuggling. In 1733, while Earl James was still alive, Walpole negotiated with Atholl over the Isle of Man, offering the British Government's recognition of the legality of his succession to the Stanley lordship as long as he agreed to sell the sovereign rights of the Island (though not his lands and other rights) to the Crown within seven years of his succession. Accordingly Atholl entered into negotiations with Britain in the years after 1736 but Walpole was obliged to concentrate on a major European War from 1739 and he resigned in 1742. However, the issue of the sale was kept alive in discussions between Atholl and Walpole's successors Henry Pelham and the Duke of Newcastle and Atholl set up a number of legal trusts in order to safeguard his

141

family's interests against the day when the sovereign rights would eventually be sold.

Although the Atholls were dukes it should not be thought that their social status, wealth or influence in Britain was greater than the Derbys and indeed Duke James took a more personal interest in the Island mainly because it was, to him, a very valuable acquisition and a potential source of considerable revenue. He was by no means just a Scottish landowner because from 1724 he held the important office of Lord Privy Seal and as such played a significant part in London politics. He visited the Island on several occasions and worked closely with the four men - all Scotsmen - whom he appointed as Governor during his 28-year rule. They were his kinsman and namesake James Murray (1736-1744), Patrick Lindesay (1744-1751), Basil Cochrane (1751-1761) and John Wood, appointed in 1761. Lindesay had been Lord Provost of Edinburgh and it is likely that they all had some military experience and perhaps links with the Scottish Excise service. They were paid about £300 a year and they lived in the Governor's apartments in Castle Rushen.

Under the Atholl regime as administered by these men from 1736 onwards there was a significant improvement in almost all aspects of Island life. In particular the House of Keys, whose members had been browbeaten on a number of occasions by the Stanley governors, were treated better. Their constitutional claims were respected and they were no longer subject to imprisonment, arbitrary dismissal or exclusion from voting, while in 1737 legislation safeguarded their right to give or withhold consent to customs legislation. By the early 1760s it had been established that the Governor would summon the Keys for legislative purposes whenever he thought fit and they met in a building on the site of the present Old House of Keys in Castletown. It was their right to elect a Speaker, to debate separately from the Governor and Council, to regulate their own sittings and to reject any Bill. Members of the Keys held office for life and when a vacancy occurred they placed two names before the Governor, who chose one of them. They were required to own landed property worth at least £3 and in general they were among the Island's richest and most influential inhabitants.

Bishop Wilson and the Manx Church were also affected by the more benevolent Atholl regime because in 1736 Tynwald reformed the ecclesiastical laws so that the number of ordinary disciplinary cases decreased and disputes between the civil and ecclesiastical courts died down and Wilson was able to devote the last years of his very long episcopate more single-mindedly to his pastoral duties. Despite his lifelong commitment to the enforcement of moral standards and religious discipline he remained extremely popular with the Manx people, largely because of his exceptional personal qualities, which included modesty, humility, generosity and respect for the poor and needy. He was also a fine speaker and an inspiring preacher. He made an effort to learn the Manx language and established libraries in the parishes and was responsible for the Manx Catechism of 1707, the first book known to have been published in Manx. He encouraged the setting up of grammar schools in Douglas, Castletown and Peel and did a great deal to re-organize and revitalize the parishes, being responsible for chapels at Castletown, St John's, Ballure, Douglas and Ramsey and churches at Lezayre, Kirk Patrick and Lonan. He repaired Bishopscourt and planted some fine trees there but he failed to prevent the cathedral from falling into permanent decay. He managed his own income well so that it rose from £300 to £400, though he gave about half of it away to charitable causes. By the time he died at Bishopscourt in 1755, aged 93, his reputation had reached far beyond the Island - which he had refused to leave, even for tempting offers such as the bishopric of Exeter - and he became the subject of several biographies, most notably that by John Keble, a leader of the nineteenth century 'Oxford Movement', who saw in Wilson's life and work the very model of Anglican sainthood.

REVESTMENT AND ITS RESULTS, 1765-1794

Duke James died in 1764, aged 74, leaving no sons, but a daughter, Charlotte. The dukedom passed to his nearest male heir, his nephew John, whereas the lordship of Man, which could descend in the female line, went to Charlotte. These first cousins had married some years before so the new Duke of Atholl became Lord of Man in right of his wife. He was not in a very strong position for this reason and also because his father had taken part in the second unsuccessful Jacobite rebellion in 1745 and had been attainted by Parliament. He therefore petitioned the Crown to permit his succession to the dukedom, and this was confirmed by a decision in the House of Lords just before his uncle died. The new duke and his wife were in their mid-thirties and they knew next to nothing about the Isle of Man.

This was the perfect moment for the British Prime Minister, **143**

George Grenville, to act decisively and win back the Island for the British Crown, a move that had been on the agenda in Westminster for over half a century. In 1764 British Treasury officials reported that the Isle of Man smuggling trade chiefly involved tea from Sweden, tobacco to and from the UK, and rum and coffee from the West Indies. Estimates of the loss in revenue to the Treasury varied from £200,000 to at least £350,000. Grenville was notorious for being pompous, long-winded and arrogant and he made two major mistakes in the short time he was in office. One was to arrest the British journalist and MP John Wilkes in 1763 using a questionably legal 'general warrant' and the other was to pass the Stamp Act of 1765 which sparked off revolt in the American colonies. His tactics regarding the Isle of Man involved reminding the new Duke of Atholl

During the Seven Years War (1756-1763) a British squadron of three ships under Captain J... of the Ballaugh coast. Elliott won a complete victory, Thurot was killed and his ships were cap... Richard Wright, a talented marine artist who happened to be on the Island at the time. The d... Manx fishing boats as well as one of the earliest representations of the Manx flag which hangs

promptly in 1764 that his title to the dukedom had depended upon Government support and that his late uncle had already contracted to sell his sovereign rights in the Isle of Man. Atholl was formally requested to state which of his rights in the Island he was prepared to sell, and for how much. It was also darkly hinted that if Atholl was not prepared to sell, the Government would consider 'other measures'. To back up this threat Parliament passed the so-called 'Mischief Act' in January 1765 which authorized British customs officials to search ships in Manx ports and punish smugglers. Faced with the possibility of a similar Act dispossessing him of his rights, Atholl agreed to sell and clutching figures from the air, to some extent, he said that he would accept £299,773 for all his rights on the Island, being £42,000 for the sovereign rights, £8,400 for the patronage of the bishopric

three French ships under Commodore Francois Thurot on 28th February 1760 within sight
the six ships were anchored in Ramsey Bay, where this fine painting was done of them by
centre is Thurot's flagship the 'Maréchal Belleisle' and the painting features square-sailed
el on the extreme lower right. (Manx National Heritage)

and church benefices and £249,373 for the customs duties, landed property and manorial rights.

At this point Grenville made the third serious error of his prime ministership because he should have accepted the figure of £299,773 and bought the Atholls out of the Island completely, thereby avoiding over sixty years of future confusion and dispute between the British Government, the Manx people and the ducal family. As it was he went for the inexpensive option and offered £46,000 for the sovereign rights and £24,000 for the customs duties, which he considered was all that was necessary to deal with the smuggling issue. As a bonus for their co-operation the Atholls also got a pension of £2,000 a year for their joint lives. All these negotiations were done over the head of the House of Keys which sent a deputation to London to safeguard the Island's interests but found itself largely ignored. Parliament quickly passed the 'Act of Revestment' which became law on May 10th 1765 and King George III, who had recently celebrated his 27th birthday, was proclaimed Lord of Man on June 21st.

The Governor of the Island since 1761 had been John Wood and the UK decided to confirm him in office to provide an element of continuity. On July 11th the Manx flag was ceremoniously lowered

The third Duke of Atholl with his family. (Manx National Heritage)

from the tower of Castle Rushen and replaced with the Union Jack, the 42nd regiment of the Black Watch fired three volleys and Governor Wood, after making a tactful speech, entertained Island dignitaries to dinner in the Castle and provided the soldiers with plenty of beer with which they were able to drink a toast to the king. Around the Island, we are told, there were 'bonfires, illuminations and demonstrations of joy'. After this Wood was more or less left to his own devices to work out how the Island should be run under the new regime because the UK did not follow up the Act of Revestment with Orders-in-Council establishing a constitution or clarifying existing structures.

George III was the Lord of Man but by this time the British king was to a great extent a constitutional monarch whose work was done by ministers and from the 1780s onwards the Isle of Man became the responsibility of the Home Secretary and remained so until the beginning of the 21st century. No definitive statement after Revestment was made on the crucial issue of what the precise relationship was to be between Parliament and Tynwald, as a result of which this has remained a debatable issue to this day. Moreover, although the Duke of Atholl was no longer sovereign Lord of the Island or responsible for the customs, he was still by far the greatest landowner and he enjoyed extensive manorial rights and also patronage in the Church, including the appointment of the bishop. So one of the main tasks of Governor Wood and his successors was to make the new regime acceptable to the Manx people and also to work out, with the Duke of Atholl and with lawyers and politicians on the Island, how the constitutional and administrative system which had been inherited in 1765 might develop in the future.

As far as the UK was concerned Wood's main priority was to clamp down on the smuggling trade by using the powers that he and the customs officials now possessed for policing shipping in Manx waters. In August 1766 the Customs Boards in London and Edinburgh ordered their officials to write reports on what the effects of the Mischief and Revestment Acts had been on Manx smuggling. Most reported that it had been virtually checked and that the stocks of contraband goods were almost exhausted, with no new importations since June 1765. There were strong indications that the trade had moved elsewhere, especially Ireland and Guernsey, with some smuggling activity direct from France, Norway and Sweden. So there was certainly an immediate and dramatic decrease in the volume of smuggling, which of course hit certain sections of the Manx community very hard.

Yet smuggling did not stop altogether and an official report of 1788 made clear that rum and salt were still being carried by Manx fishing boats to secret destinations on the UK's north-west coast while Irish boats took sugar and wine to Ireland and contraband brandy and gin were consumed by the Island's inhabitants. Another report in 1791 argued that smuggling would never be stopped altogether without a substantial increase in the number of active and determined revenue vessels working together with military forces stationed on the Island. A degree of smuggling therefore remained a factor until changes in the customs duties in the next century made the trade less worthwhile. It can nevertheless be said that the scale of smuggling was reduced dramatically soon after Revestment and that the UK thereby substantially achieved its main purpose in resuming control over the Island in 1765.

Under Governor Wood the number of members of the Council was reduced from twelve to five and Englishmen rather than Manxmen were appointed to important positions, such as Sir Wadsworth Busk, who was appointed Attorney-General in 1774 and Richard Dawson who became Wood's deputy, as Lieutenant Governor, in 1775. The next year Bishop Richmond noted that 'since Revestment the people have been much concerned as to how their laws were made - by the Keys or by Parliament. Lt Governor Dawson by obtaining the royal assent to those [laws] framed by the Keys has solved the question'. This royal assent to Manx legislation was an important constitutional development which is still very much part of Manx legislative practice today. When Wood died in 1777 he was replaced by a soldier, Edward Smith, who held office for sixteen years and was eventually promoted major-general, though he was often away attending to military duties in the UK such as helping to quell the Gordon Riots in London in 1780. During his absence his work was done by Dawson, who with Busk continued to make progress in establishing a stable form of government on the Island.

This promising situation was upset in 1774 by the premature death of the third Duke of Atholl, who was only in his mid-forties. He was succeeded by his eldest son John, the fourth duke, who was still in his twenties and who was convinced that his father had died of a broken heart over being forced to sell the lordship of the Island, and for such a modest sum. This was the new duke's interpretation of events,

King George III. (Manx National Heritage)

though it seems that his father actually died of drowning while suffering delusions after an apoplectic fit. Nevertheless, the fourth duke came to an early decision that he would make it his life's work to attempt to recover as much as possible of what his father had lost. His first step was to claim manorial dues which had not been paid since 1765 and Dawson and Busk countered with legislation in the Keys to reduce his manorial rights where possible. In 1781 Atholl introduced a Bill in Parliament to amend the Revestment Act on the grounds that his father had been paid far too little for the customs rights and Sir George Moore, increasingly described as the 'Speaker' of the House of Keys, travelled to London to argue against it so successfully that the Bill was dropped. Ten years later Atholl petitioned the Crown to appoint a Royal Commission to inquire into his many grievances in the Isle of Man and in 1792 the Commission reported that on the whole they agreed with the duke's general assertion that his father had been paid too little and that his manorial rights had been infringed by Tynwald. Atholl's response was to request that he should be appointed Governor of the Island at the first opportunity, not for the salary, which was trivial by his standards, but so that he could stop attempts by the Council and Keys to erode his position as a great landowner on the Island and perhaps attempt to recoup his father's losses where possible.

THE MANX BIBLE AND THE ARRIVAL OF METHODISM

When Bishop Wilson died in 1755 he was replaced by Mark Hildesley who had been born in 1698 and educated at Charterhouse and Trinity College, Cambridge, where he was subsequently elected to a fellowship. In 1731 he became Vicar of Hitchin and continued to hold this living after his appointment to the Isle of Man. He embraced the life and culture of his adopted Island with vigour and was responsible for the renovation of several parish churches and the construction of St Mark's, Malew, and St George's, Douglas, both necessary because the existing churches were often full to overflowing. Above all Hildesley came to the conclusion that because most of the 20,000 or so inhabitants of the Island spoke Manx Gaelic, it was essential that the Bible and Prayer Book should be translated into the Island's native language. He was not a fluent Manx speaker himself but he called upon the assistance of a number of Manx scholars, especially Philip Moore and John Kelly, who with the assistance of the SPCK in London were able to publish the four gospels and the Acts of the Apostles in 1763, the Book of Common Prayer in 1765, the second part of the New Testament in 1767, the first part of the Old Testament in 1771 and the second in 1773. By then Hildesley had died in November 1772, having suffered a stroke the day after his last sermon, on the uncertainty of life.

Hildesley was a profuse letter-writer and a kindly humorist, greatly loved by his many friends and the Manx people at large. Much as he liked the Island, however, he was conscious of being cut off from the centre of things. He loved British newspapers but by the time he received them they had been through many hands and were long out of date and he wrote in one of his letters that 'Though we are within sight of the three kingdoms of His Majesty of Britain, I believe we often know less of what happen in [them] than some do in America'. Even a journey on the very poor roads from Douglas to Kirk Michael he described as 'crossing the Alps' or the Pyrenees. Nor was there even a postal service on the Island at this time and his letters had to be carried by friends bound for the same destination.

As a result of the exceptional popularity of bishops Wilson and Hildesley, together with Wilson's strenuous efforts to combat immorality, it seems likely that Anglicanism in the Isle of Man was in a more healthy state than in Britain at large where religious observance had become lax and 'enthusiasm' was frowned upon. This prompted John Wesley, a High Church, High Tory, Anglican clergyman, to lead an evangelical movement - later nicknamed 'Methodism'- which held open-air meetings where fiery sermons stirred up the relatively simple souls who listened to them. Eventually the Methodists were considered outsiders and treated with hostility by the church authorities. The Methodist John Murlin visited Ramsey in 1758 by mistake, having boarded the wrong ship at Whitehaven. He stayed a week and preached in a barn which proved to be too small for the Sunday service which he held out of doors. His audience behaved well and paid close attention but he felt ultimately that there was 'little probability of doing any considerable good while the whole Island was a nest of smugglers'. Many years passed until the Liverpool Methodists sent John Crook to the Island in 1775 and he met with considerable success, repeated the following year. However, Bishop Hildesley's successor Richard Richmond, considered a haughty and overbearing man, strongly discouraged his clergy from helping the Methodists though the new Governor, Edward Smith, seemed well disposed to them.

Wesley himself made the first of two visits to the Island in 1777. He was by then aged 74, a small, neat, fresh-coloured man with his hair well-combed. When giving his outdoor sermons in all the main towns he spoke quickly, making use of much factual material and eloquence, and often ending on a theatrical note. He was impressed with the Manx, declaring that 'a more loving, simple-hearted people than this I never saw. And no wonder, for they have but six papists and no dissenters in the Island'. From 1778 the Island was deemed to be a separate Methodist circuit and the number of followers increased rapidly from about 600 in 1778 to 1,597 in 1781. In that year Wesley made a second visit, preaching in Douglas, Castletown and Peel where he found 'the largest congregation I have seen in the Island'. He also preached in the open air on South Barrule so convincingly that 18-year-old William Faragher from Cooilcam, who died in 1856, became 'convinced of sin' and entered himself upon a life of Methodist evangelism.

Wesley visited the graves of Wilson and Hildesley at Kirk Michael but found the Island 'shut up from the world and having little trade ....visited by scarce any strangers'. The Manx he considered 'a plain, artless, simple people; unpolished, that is, unpolluted; few of them

Bishop Mark Hildesley. (Manx National Heritage)

are rich or genteel; the far greater part moderately poor; and most of the strangers that settle among them are men that have seen affliction. The local preachers are men of faith and love, knit together in one mind and one judgement. They speak either Manx or English, and follow a regular plan'. In 1789 a Methodist preacher, George Holder, suggested the publication of a hymn book in Manx Gaelic, but he got a frosty response from Wesley: 'I exceedingly disapprove of your publishing anything in the Manx language. On the contrary, we should do everything in our power to abolish it from the earth and persuade every member of our Society to learn and talk English'.

THE GOVERNORSHIP OF THE FOURTH DUKE OF ATHOLL, 1793-1830

Atholl's request to be appointed Governor of the Isle of Man was speedily granted because, as it happened, General Edward Smith died in 1793 and the post became vacant. The position of Governor, though obviously important within the Isle of Man, was hardly a glittering prize, commanding a comparatively modest salary and with somewhat draughty accommodation within Castle Rushen. Over the centuries during which the Stanleys had been Lords they had usually appointed as Governors Lancashire or Cheshire men from the lesser gentry, often with military experience, and junior members of the Stanley family sometimes held the post. Few Governors had been men of distinction or even prominence in a British context and it was unprecedented for someone who was a duke and a great landowner to accept the position. Clearly Atholl had a dream of somehow using his powers as Governor, together with his other rights and properties on the Island, to recoup family losses and he even hoped to use his considerable political influence in London to have the Revestment Act overturned.

If evidence is needed of the Duke's grand vision for a new Atholl regime on the Island, it is not necessary to look further than his miniature palace, Castle Mona. Although the Governors had traditionally occupied a residence in Castle Rushen, General Smith was absent a great deal and his house was occupied by his deputy, Richard Dawson, and from 1790 by Dawson's successor Alexander Shaw. First of all Atholl bought a house on the North Quay in Douglas (now the Douglas Hotel), and then a property at Port-e-Chee and he also considered building new apartments in Peel Castle, but found the whole site too seriously decayed. Eventually he commissioned a

Scottish architect, George Steuart, to build a new mansion house in the classical style of Robert Adam close to the sea shore, near Douglas. It was built in white stone imported from Arran and contained grand public rooms, luxuriously decorated and furnished. The cost was amazingly high - £36,000 - which was half of what his father had received for the lordship and customs duties. When invited guests attended the lavish opening party in August 1804 they could not but admire the most impressive private house ever built on the Island. Given that the expense caused financial problems for him, that he seldom used the house, that his long-term plans for a revival of the Atholl lordship never worked out and that it was sold for less than half the cost price as a hotel soon after his death, the whole project must be seen as extravagant and unwise.

In his defence it must be said that Atholl was keen to bring about several important improvements to the Island's infrastructure and soon after he became Governor he commissioned George Steuart to construct the 'Red Pier' in Douglas harbour. About 158 metres long by 12 wide, it was opened at the turn of the century and it had the added bonus of serving as a promenade, very popular with the upper classes of Douglas in fine weather. Atholl also had plans to construct new Court Houses at Castle Rushen and Kirk Michael, a new House of Keys at Castletown and prisons for Douglas, Peel and Ramsey, though none of these went beyond the drawing-board stage.

Meanwhile Atholl kept up the pressure on the UK government to be given compensation for Revestment. He sent a petition with a long list of grievances to the Privy Council in 1801 but after much delay it was rejected in March 1804. In May Atholl's political ally William Pitt the Younger returned to Downing Street and made sure that another petition was successful. Accordingly an Act of Parliament in 1805 awarded Atholl and his heirs in perpetuity an annual payment equal to a quarter of the gross annual customs of the Island, as compensation for the Revestment Act. This extremely generous decision, which involved handing over to Atholl a sum of about £3,000 a year, was made against the advice of several committees of the Lords, Commons and Privy Council and seems to have been the result of Pitt's personal influence and regarded by critics as grossly corrupt. Another provision of this Act was bad news for the Island because it stipulated that in future all Manx revenues should be counted as part of the British Treasury's general income and should not be reserved for specifically Manx purposes. The result of this was that for the next sixty years it was in the interests of the UK government to keep investment in the Isle of Man down to a minimum while extracting as much as possible from it in terms of customs and other revenue.

Buoyed up by this success Atholl attempted to strengthen his position on the Island by securing the appointment of administrators loyal to himself. In 1796 he had proposed a Scotsman, Charles Hope, as Attorney General but the Home Office had told him firmly that it was not his job as Governor to make such appointments. When Alexander Shaw resigned in 1804 Atholl promptly appointed his younger brother Lord Henry Murray as Lieutenant Governor but this was also vetoed by the Home Office which again pointed out that Atholl was exceeding his powers. Instead they appointed Colonel Cornelius Smelt to the position, thus beginning a long-running contest between Atholl and his official deputy. Smelt was an Englishman who had fought in the American War of Independence and he was considered an old soldier and gentleman of the old school – composed, discreet, courteous, affable, firm and resolute.

Smelt was not overawed by Atholl and irritated him in a number of ways. First, he refused to lend Atholl his Castle Rushen residence when the Duke was on the Island attending to official duties in Castletown, which meant that he had either to make the bumpy journey on bad roads back to Castle Mona, or stay overnight at an inn. Both parties appealed over this issue to the Home Office, which backed Smelt. Second, Smelt tended to support the House of Keys in their policy of resisting Atholl's attempts to increase the revenue from his tenants - which many of the Keys actually were. Also, Atholl frequently complained that Smelt often acted without consulting him, which was true enough but inevitable given that Atholl was essentially an absentee Governor, visiting the Island only four times between 1805 and 1821, for instance. Hence a situation gradually developed whereby the Island was administered by a popular Lieutenant Governor who was often in dispute with his increasingly unpopular and absentee superior.

In 1814 Atholl, making use of his inherited right to appoint the bishop, chose his nephew George Murray for the post. Once he had overcome his dismay at the dilapidated state of Bishopscourt, Murray proved a loyal ally to his uncle and in 1822 he wrote to the Home Secretary, Sir Robert Peel, attempting to persuade him to set up a Royal Commission to inquire into the government of the Island. He complained that the Keys were self-elected and that too many of them were related to each other, that they were encouraged by Smelt to resist the authority of Atholl, that they frequently gave unjust judgements in disputes about property, and that they met in an illegal manner and in private. In fact the Keys had just moved into the newly built 'Old House of Keys' building in Castletown, but Atholl had little respect for their claims to represent the Manx people, taking the view that they were nothing more than a rich, self-perpetuating oligarchy and famously telling them on one occasion that they were no more representative of the people of Man than of the people of Peru. Peel no doubt noted Bishop Murrays's criticisms but he did not set up the requested Commission. In 1823 Atholl complained to the UK that the Keys had begun to misuse their appellate role in the Court of General Gaol Delivery to the point of voting on every case and in 1825 the Privy Council ruled that the Keys should restrict their activities to being a Court of Appeal only.

Eventually Atholl and the bishop took a step too far when in 1825 they decided to revive a lapsed right to claim payment of tithes on green crops, fixing the charge at twelve shillings an acre - which was four times the similar charge in Ireland and nearly five times that in the north of England. This provoked nothing less than open rebellion

The fourth Duke of Atholl with his family. (Manx National Heritage)

and about 3,000 people with bludgeons and pitchforks concealed under their coats descended on Castle Rushen where the bishop and his family had taken refuge. Lieutenant Governor Smelt acted as mediator, persuading the crowd to disperse in return for a promise that the bishop would agree to cancel the tithe. When the people discovered that the tithe had been cancelled for one year only, they rioted again and marched on Bishopscourt. The tithe scheme had to be abandoned and by 1827 Murray had left the Island to become Bishop of Rochester.

Atholl himself had not been on the Island during these troubles but soon afterwards he came to the decision that he would never be able to recreate an Atholl lordship in Man and decided to offer the British Government all his remaining rights there for the considerable sum of £417,144. This was in addition to about £70,000 which he had already received according to the agreement in 1805 which paid him £3,000 a year. Atholl's offer was accepted in1829 after which time he remained an absentee Governor only while his inherited claims to ecclesiastical patronage, mining rights, lands, quit-rents, alienation fees and other dues were all transferred to the Crown. Having received total payments amounting to nearly half a million pounds Atholl had in fact succeeded in gaining financial compensation for Revestment, and as stated earlier, the UK would have done far better to have paid his father £299,773 for his entire rights in 1765. Atholl invested a great deal of personal interest and effort in the Island but it is hard to deny that the main motive for it was to increase his own revenues and improve his family's position. His decision to give up on the Island was partially influenced by the sad fact that his heir suffered from mental illness and would not be capable of looking after the family's affairs there. Atholl himself died in 1830, aged 75, and the dukedom remained in the main line of his family until 1957, when it passed to a distant kinsman. Castle Mona was sold for the bargain price of £16,000 in 1831 to a consortium led by a Manxman, Captain Caesar Bacon, who turned it into a hotel. Ironically, in the circumstances, Bacon's wife was the daughter of Cornelius Smelt.

AGRICULTURE, FISHING AND MINING

Although the Isle of Man has proved to be comparatively rich in zinc, lead and copper, a crucial factor in its development has been a complete lack of coal. This meant that the Island never became an industrialized community from the late eighteenth century onwards, when the so-called 'Industrial Revolution' took hold in Britain and transformed the UK into the world's greatest power during the nineteenth century. Moreover, as we have seen, the Manx never established themselves as successful mercantile traders, partly as a result of heavy restrictions on trade imposed by the Stanley lords. Therefore until the tourist trade became established in the late nineteenth century the Island relied mainly on its historic industries of agriculture, fishing and mining together with the 'running trade'.

John Meyrick, who was both Bishop and Governor, gave one of the earliest assessments of Manx agriculture in 1577 when he said that it was rich in flocks and corn though more from the hard work of the Manx people than the richness of the soil. Still, at that time there was surplus produce and a good deal was exported. Oats were the chief food of the people, with potatoes also plentiful. Manx cattle were of poor stature though the sheep were fat and tasty to eat. Manx horses were sooty black in colour with long, straggling hair and they were hardy but small and rather ugly. From 1660 to 1704 agriculture fell into decline because of the uncertainties of the straw tenure dispute and many workers turned to fishing instead. Writers during the seventeenth century remarked on the scarcity of trees in the Island and in the 1720s it was reported that a man might ride many miles and see nothing but a thorn tree with a fence round it to protect such a rarity. Bishop Wilson planted trees with enthusiasm but it was not until the nineteenth century that systematic attempts were made at plantation. A notable improvement to the usefulness of the landscape took place between 1756 and 1776 with the draining of the Curragh marshes in the northern plain.

The overall agricultural situation was still unsatisfactory at Revestment in 1765 and the UK attempted to improve conditions by encouraging the Island to import wheat, barley, oats, meal and flour. The Duke of Atholl still regarded Manx agriculture as backward in 1792 but the establishment of the Workington Agricultural Society in the Island in 1807 led to improvements in the breeding and management of livestock, though agricultural implements were still primitive and even horse-drawn carts rare. Between 1808 and 1816 there was a burst of prosperity owing to the arrival of English incomers and also the presence of numerous military troops during the Napoleonic War with France but after peace was declared in 1815 there soon came a depression caused by the withdrawal of the troops and several bad harvests, together with demands for the payment of old and new tithes. So serious was the position that many Manx labourers emigrated to America between 1825 and 1837.

To some extent the lack of progress in agriculture was blamed on the fact that many labourers turned away from the fields in July, August and September in order to go fishing. From the earliest times fish had been a ready source of food for the Manx and as early as 1261 the Church claimed a tithe on all fish caught, while the Lord was entitled to one fish out of every five. In 1610 the Island's Statutes considered that the herring fishery was 'as great a blessing as this poor Island receives' and it was subject to tight restrictions, supervised by the water-bailiff. In 1670 there were about 200 Manx fishing boats in use and 415 by 1777, having one mast and a square sail though the 'wherry' rig was then developed with two masts and a sail fore and aft. From about 1830 the 'dandy' or 'yawl' rig became the norm and by 1800 about 2,500 men and boys were involved in fishing. From time to time, however, the usually plentiful shoals of herring did not appear in Manx waters for reasons which have never been fully explained. The first recorded failure was in 1612 and there were others around 1648 and 1687 and between 1700 and 1710, with a long gap until another serious failure in 1827.

Mining is first mentioned in 1246 when King Harald granted the monks of Furness Abbey the rights to work the Island's lead and iron mines. Around 1650 Captain Edward Christian discovered that the rocks at Bradda Head contained silver, but it was lead and copper that were chiefly mined at Foxdale and Laxey. Bishop Wilson wrote in the early eighteenth century that on the Island 'mines of coal are there none, though several attempts have been made to find them, but of lead, copper, and iron, there are several and some of them have been wrought to good advantage, especially the lead; of which ore many hundred tons have of late been smelted and exported'. During the rest of the century the mines were not fully exploited but from 1823 there was vigorous activity at both Foxdale and Laxey, where rich new veins were discovered, and an iron mine was opened at Maughold in 1837. The Island may have missed out on an industrial revolution, but wily entrepreneurs were beginning to see that there might be a lot of money to be made from mining in the future.

Chapter Twelve
Constitutional and Economic progress, 1830-1914

AFTER ATHOLL 1830-1868

Even though Cornelius Smelt was aged 83 when the Duke of Atholl died he hoped to be appointed Governor with an increased salary to go with the title and he wrote letters to the Home Office pleading poverty brought about by the expenses of his position. In fact the Home Office gave him the full responsibility of a Governor but only with the title and salary of Lieutenant Governor. This may have been because they had had such a difficult time with the 'overmighty' Atholl that they wished to downgrade the post to some extent. Smelt did not have long to live but in April 1830 he presided over an impressive ceremony to lay the foundation stone of King William's College. This was attended by 5,000 people including a band which played 'See the Conquering Hero Comes' as Smelt made his appearance. The building of the school was mainly the result of the efforts of Bishop William Ward who was able to release the accumulated funds originally set aside in the 1660s by Bishop Barrow and also raise £4,000, half by public subscriptions and half by mortgages. The College opened in 1833 and it has played an important part in Island life ever since, educating many Manx children as well as pupils from abroad. Smelt died in November 1832 and in 1835 the public began to subscribe to a tribute to him in the shape of a fine classical column, which stands in Castletown opposite the entrance to the Castle and remains the only significant memorial to one of the Island's Governors. The architect was John Welch, who also designed the Tower of Refuge in Douglas Bay.

To succeed Smelt the Home Office appointed Colonel (later Major-General) John Ready, an experienced administrator who had been Lieutenant Governor of Prince Edward Island in Canada (where there was a Governor-General who was his superior). However, he was appointed to the Isle of Man with the title of Lieutenant Governor and not Governor, and that title has been used ever since. The fact that a Lieutenant Governor is usually the deputy of a Governor has been cheerfully and consistently overlooked. Nevertheless on the Island the

Crown's representative has often been referred to as 'the Governor', as he will be sometimes in this account. Ready's overall task was to keep the Isle of Man as tranquil as possible and also to eradicate what was left of the smuggling trade in order that increased Manx revenues would reach London and return to the Treasury some of the £417,144 it had been forced to pay the Duke of Atholl.

In 1832 the British Parliament passed its 'Great Reform Act', the first of three Acts during the nineteenth century which gradually made the House of Commons more representative of the British people. The following year the influential Manx radical Robert Fargher founded *The Mona's Herald* on the Isle of Man as a newspaper which became the main organ of a growing movement demanding political reform. In 1836 the UK government told Ready that it intended to bring the Island's customs duties into line with those in England, partly to kill off what was left of the smuggling and partly to raise more revenue. This produced a storm of protest on the Island, largely whipped up by Fargher and his supporters. The low customs duties had been greatly beneficial to the Manx economy over the preceding forty years because the lower cost of living had attracted the first 'come-overs' from the UK. These were mostly retired army and naval officers on pensions which went much further on the Island than in Britain. It was they who built themselves the fine classical-style houses and terraces

King William's College. (Miles Cowsill)

which still grace parts of central Douglas, and the population of the town rose from about 2,000 in 1765 to about 9,000 in 1845. The total population of the Island also swelled from around 28,000 in 1792 to nearly 42,000 in 1831, though it was then reduced by a number of serious cholera outbreaks.

The British proposals to change the customs duties did not go ahead in the 1830s as planned but the threat remained and to combat it Fargher and his colleagues turned their fire on the House of Keys. They quoted Sir Robert Peel's view that it was 'so anomalous a body as could not exist within the British Empire' and argued that it should be reformed so that it would be held in greater esteem and carry more weight in negotiations to protect Manx interests. A petition for an elected House of Keys received 3,000 signatures in 1838 but it came at a bad time for Britain, which was having colonial difficulties with the governments of Canada and Jamaica and was not keen to sanction a semi-autonomous elected parliament on the Isle of Man. Another blow came in 1844 when Peel, by then Prime Minister, did increase the Manx customs duties (though not to yet the UK's level). He balanced this to some extent by abolishing the existing licence system which had allowed a small number of English merchants to dominate the Manx import trade and by giving £2,300 a year out of the new customs duties to be spent on improvements to the Island's harbours. One significant result of the increase in customs duties was the Island's reduced attractiveness as a place to live for the pensioned 'genteel' classes, some of whom returned to the UK.

In 1845 Ready died, aged 73, when he accidently swallowed poison instead of medicine and he was succeeded by the Hon. Charles Hope, a young Scottish aristocrat and former MP who soon reported back to London that he saw no need for reform of the Keys and considered that the reform party was largely powered by a few articulate individuals and did not have much popular support. In 1847 reformers pounced on the fact that the Keys, sitting as an appeal court, had granted libel damages to the client of George Dumbell, who was one of the members of the Keys himself and had sat in judgement for the appeal. The reformers put the case before the Home Secretary, Sir George Grey, but backed down quickly when Grey suggested that the best solution to the anomalies of the Keys was the complete incorporation of the Isle of Man into the United Kingdom. In 1853 the Keys, probably inspired by the Chartist movement in the UK, again made demands for greater control over the Island's revenue but Hope advised the Home Office to resist on the grounds that the Keys would not be likely to overcome personal and local interests when disposing of large sums of money. The UK's response was to increase the harbour improvement grant of 1844 to £3,411 but to pay for this the duties on spirits and tobacco were at last raised to the UK level, which was a strong countermeasure to whatever smuggling practices were still in operation.

The Manx economy faltered between 1830 and the 1860s. There had been a good run of harvests in the 1830s and the foundation of the Manx Agricultural Society in 1840 renewed enthusiasm for new farming methods but a disease destroyed potatoes in 1845 and 1846, leading to another wave of emigration to America and Australia. In 1860 the Disafforesting Act, prompted by the recommendations of a Royal Commission, redistributed common land leaving the mountain crofters with far less pasture freely available for their animals. After unsuccessful protests many of them moved to work in the towns and the Manx uplands increasingly became dotted with deserted cottages (tholtans). Fishing was hit from 1823 onwards by competition from as many as 300 Cornish boats, from the removal in 1833 of the bounty on herrings paid by the UK and from the abolition of slavery which reduced the West Indian market for cured herrings. By the 1840s the Manx fishing fleet was down to about 220 vessels, operated by 1,500 men. The only economic success story was mining and the Foxdale and Laxey mines produced unprecedented quantities of ore in the 1850s, making great profits for their shareholders. There was also a modest growth in manufacturing from a cottage industry in 1800 to a small factory-based industry producing woollen cloth and sailcloth in Douglas and Union Mills. Shipbuilding also grew steadily after the first large yard was established in Douglas in 1828. There were four yards in Castletown by the 1850s and the yard at Ramsey employed 250 men in 1863 and was capable of building wooden or iron ships up to 2,000 tons.

This period also saw the foundation of the Isle of Man Steam Packet Company, which was to be so vital a part of Island life. The first British steamer was built in 1812 and seven years later a steamship service was established between Liverpool and Glasgow, calling at Douglas. In 1822 the St George Steam Packet Company from Liverpool also worked this route and in 1830 a number of Manx businessmen formed the Mona's Isle Company, named after its first steamboat. In 1830 the *St George* was wrecked on Conister Rock and Sir William Hillary, a

Douglas resident, rowed out with volunteers to save the crew. He subsequently raised money to build the Tower of Refuge on Conister Rock, completed in 1832, and a lighthouse was built on Douglas Head in the same year. Later on Hillary won a secure place in British maritime history through being the main force behind the foundation of the Royal National Lifeboat Institution. The wreck of the *St George* put its company out of business and in 1831 the Mona's Isle Company took over its mail contract, worth £1,000 a year, and changed its name to the Isle of Man Steam Packet Company in 1832. In its early years the company ran wooden and iron paddle steamers named *King Orry*, *Ben-my-Chree* and *Tynwald* and carried some 20,000 passengers a year. In 1858 the *Douglas*, which was considered to be the fastest steamer afloat, joined the fleet and made the crossing from Liverpool to Douglas in four hours and twenty minutes. By the 1860s the Steam Packet was in a dominant position and poised to expand in a spectacular way to cope with the developing tourist industry.

Governor Hope is chiefly remembered on the Island for two incidents. One occurred in 1847 when the Royal Yacht unexpectedly arrived in Ramsey Bay on September 20th. It contained Queen Victoria, Prince Albert and their children, who had been enjoying a cruise on the west coast of Scotland. As the water was choppy the Queen stayed on board while Prince Albert went ashore in a small boat and had a good look round Ramsey, climbing to where the Albert

Copy of a drawing of Charles Hope, Lady Isabella Hope and son John by artist Jemima Wedderbush, part of a visual diary of a Victorian lady. (Manx National Heritage)

Tower now stands above Ballure Glen. Meanwhile Hope was making frantic efforts to reach Ramsey on the poor roads from Castletown, but by the time he arrived the royal pair had sailed on, presumably to have a look at Douglas Bay before crossing to the newly developed port of Fleetwood and travelling from there to London on the equally new railway network. Hope was blamed by the Manx for failing to greet the Queen on what was the first visit of a reigning British sovereign to the Island, but it was hardly his fault. The other, more happy, incident was the ceremonial opening of the Laxey Wheel in September 1854, the largest of its kind in Europe. Designed by Robert Casement of Lezayre it had been built to pump water out of the lead mines, which were enjoying a boom period under the leadership of the dynamic businessman George Dumbell. According to the local press, between three and four thousand people arrived to see Hope set the wheel in motion and it was christened 'Lady Isabella' in honour of his wife, a daughter of the Earl of Selkirk.

Hope chose to retire in 1860 and he was replaced by Francis Pigott, formerly MP for Reading. His arrival on the Island was given prominent coverage in the *Illustrated London News*, complete with engravings of his ship sailing into Douglas Bay, and this suggests that the Isle of Man was beginning to be seen in London as far less of a backwater. Rejecting the inadequate Governor's quarters in Castle Rushen, both Ready and Hope had leased the elegant Lorne House in Castletown but Pigott immediately made a decision which had far-reaching consequences. He determined that Government House should be in Douglas and he rented the Villa Marina, then a Regency-style house on Douglas Bay. He also announced that it would be his policy in due course to move both Tynwald and the Law Courts from Castletown to Douglas, which was now by far the dominant town. This of course infuriated the residents of Castletown and delighted those in Douglas. Sadly Pigott died in 1863, probably from cancer, and his plans were put on hold for the moment.

HENRY LOCH AND HIS SUCCESSORS 1868-1914

Hope had been 37 on his appointment but Henry Loch was only 36, though he looked older because he was the proud owner of a long and shaggy beard. Another Scot, he had joined the navy as a boy before serving with the army in the Crimea, travelling to most parts of the world and gaining a reputation for heroism after his capture by the Chinese in 1860 during Lord Elgin's advance on Tientsin. He returned

The 'Queen of the Isle' served the Isle of Man Steam Packet Company between 1834-1844. (Ferry Publications Library)

to England and became private secretary to the Home Secretary, Sir George Grey, who was so impressed with him that, despite his youth and inexperience, he appointed him Lieutenant Governor of the Island on Pigott's death. His suitability for the post was much increased by his marriage in 1862 to a nineteen-year old beauty, Elizabeth Villiers, the niece of Lord Clarendon, another senior politician. Loch lost no time in deciding to continue Pigott's policy of shifting the political and legal balance on the Island from Castletown to Douglas. He chose not to live in the Villa Marina but he rented another large house, Bemahague, in Onchan, which has remained Government House ever since. In due course Tynwald moved first to the Douglas Court House and then in 1879 to the present 'wedding-cake' building on Prospect Hill, formerly the Bank of Mona, and a new Tynwald chamber was built next to it in 1894.

Loch's next step was to solve, by clever diplomacy, the two problems which had bedevilled Manx politics since 1830, the demands for democratic elections to the House of Keys and some degree of control for Tynwald over the spending of Manx revenues. In 1864 the Keys took exception to criticisms of them that appeared in the *Isle of Man Times* and they summoned the editor, James Brown, to the bar of the Keys and committed him to prison for six months for contempt of the House. Brown appealed and a Court presided over by Loch ruled that the Keys had no right to imprison for contempt and awarded Brown considerable damages. This episode no doubt persuaded Loch that some reform of the Keys was overdue. His chance came when in 1865 a storm destroyed an uncompleted breakwater in Douglas harbour for which Tynwald had borrowed £45,000, so it was now faced with a serious financial crisis. On his own initiative Loch persuaded the UK government to allow Tynwald control over any surplus Manx revenues in return for which Tynwald would agree to the raising of customs duties in line with the UK and also the introduction of elections to the House of Keys.

These principles were accepted by both sides and enshrined in the Isle of Man Customs and Harbours Act of 1866 which substantially raised customs duties and required Tynwald to pay £10,000 a year to cover military, defence and other expenses. Any revenue remaining could be spent by Tynwald, but only subject to the agreement of the British Treasury and the veto of the Governor. The rate of the customs duties in the future was to be set by the UK, which would also determine the salaries of officials and the overall cost of government. This arrangement was not quite the 'Home Rule' for the Island that was sometimes claimed and many agreed with William Callister MHK who complained to the *Manx Sun*, 'It just comes to this, that we are to spend the money just as they [the UK] tell us, and the idea that the representatives of the Island will have the right to expend it is all moonshine'. However, it was still a very important step towards self-government which provided a good base for exploitation by Tynwald in the years to come.

The House of Keys duly passed a Bill on December 20th 1866 which at last made the House an elected assembly. The Island was divided into ten electoral districts consisting of the towns of Peel, Ramsey and Castletown, with one member each, Douglas with three members, and the sheadings of Glenfaba, Michael, Ayre, Garff, Middle and Rushen with three members each. Voters had to be males over 21 who were owners of real estate worth at least eight pounds, or tenants paying rent of twelve pounds. The first Manx general election took place in April 1867 and resulted in the return of 13 of the 24 members of the previous House of Keys, with the 11 new members being for the most part equally conservative by temperament. In 1867 the Keys lost its ancient role as an appellate body when Tynwald's Appellate Jurisdiction Act set up a new Court of Appeal. In 1881 the vote was given to spinsters and widows, which made the Island one of the first democratic communities in the world to enfranchise women - 37 years before the UK. In 1892, as a result of the rapid expansion of Douglas, the town was divided into the electoral districts of North Douglas (three members) and South Douglas (two), while the less populated sheadings of Garff and Michael lost one member each. Further adjustments of the electoral districts have been made subsequently to account for population growth, especially in Onchan.

Another of Loch's contributions towards the transformation of the Isle of Man was his determination that it should cease to be a quiet fishing, mining and agricultural community with a few hundred expatriate Britons enjoying a less expensive standard of living in Douglas. Instead it should become a major holiday destination for the working-class people of north-western England and Scotland and Ireland. The rapid expansion of the railway network in Britain in the 1840s and 1850s had led to the growth of many seaside resorts, of which Blackpool was one of the most successful, and Loch realized that with the help of the Steam Packet Company's vessels sailing from Fleetwood and Liverpool, Douglas could become a major rival. In 1873 the Victoria Pier was opened in Douglas harbour, enabling ships to tie up alongside instead of having to anchor in the Bay, and in Loch's first ten years the number of visitors coming to the Island rose from 60,000 a year to 90,000. The next priority was to improve amenities in Douglas itself and Victoria Street opened in 1875, as did the new 'Loch Parade' on the seafront. The impressive Villiers Hotel was built at one end while the rest was filled with scores of terraced boarding houses. Loch also fought hard to achieve harbour improvements in Peel, Ramsey, Port St Mary and Port Erin and he was a strong supporter of the development of a railway system on the Island.

In 1870 the Isle of Man Steam Railway was registered and one of its main investors was the fabulously rich Duke of Sutherland, a railway enthusiast with whom Loch had family connections. The first line was built along the central valley from Douglas to Peel and the engineer, Henry Vignoles, decided to use a narrow three-feet gauge. It was opened by the Duke with great celebration in July 1873. A more difficult and expensive route from Douglas to Port Erin via Castletown opened the following year but proved so costly to the company that they contemplated no further expansion for the time being. This left Ramsey isolated so some businessmen from the north of the Island formed a company which opened a line from St John's to Ramsey via the north-west coast in 1879 and this had the effect of linking all the major towns by rail. The economic consequences of this were immediate because it was now possible for Ramsey, Peel, Port St Mary and Port Erin to join in the tourist boom and over the next decade or so terraces of hotels and seaside promenades sprang up in all these locations.

Loch's reforming activities ranged widely over many other aspects of the Island's life. In the late 1860s a number of Acts brought Manx legal practice up to date in areas such as petty sessions, the criminal code, limited liability, wills and the registration of deeds. Loch followed the UK's Education Act of 1870 with an Act in 1872 which set up a Manx Board of Education and divided the Island into school districts as well as ordering compulsory attendance at school, though there was strong resistance to this at first, especially in the countryside. He set up a Commission of Inquiry into the condition of the poor in 1878 and would have liked to establish a new hospital but found little support for it. After much political manoeuvering he managed to settle the debt owed to the UK for a failed harbour harbour scheme in Port Erin and instead funded improvements in Peel, Port St Mary and Ramsey. He also introduced a daily mail service. Despite his strength of character, determination and skill he did not always manage to overcome conservative opposition to his reforms in the Keys,which shows that the reformed House was learning how to flex its muscles: some MHKs, notably Richard Sherwood, were prepared to stand up to him. For instance, Loch regarded the Island's bishopric as too small to be viable and recommended that it be included within the new diocese of Liverpool but Tynwald would not hear of it. Loch also felt that the bishop's emoluments (once notoriously niggardly) had grown too large and they were reduced from £2,500 to £2,000 a year – still ahead of Loch's own salary of £1,500.

After nineteen years, and with a knighthood for his efforts, Loch - who must be the main contender for the title of the Island's most successful and important Governor - left in 1882 and soon became Governor of Victoria, in Australia, and then Governor of Cape Colony in South Africa: meanwhile his wife's sister became Vicereine of India. He was created Baron Loch of Drylaw in 1895 and died in 1900, aged 73. Spencer Walpole, his successor on the Isle of Man, was a far less flamboyant personality. Descended from the great Sir Robert Walpole he was also the grandson of another Prime Minister, Spencer Perceval, and his father was three times Home Secretary. Walpole himself

Sir Henry Loch. (Manx National Heritage)

became a senior civil servant and he was also a notable historian. He was at first considered a disappointment by the Manx, who had become accustomed to the larger-than-life personality of Loch, but Walpole's more quiet and scholarly approach eventually won their confidence. Under him the policies begun by Loch were continued and in the 1887 season there were 347,968 passenger arrivals in Douglas, which continued to expand as a seaside town. In Ramsey the Queen's Pier was built in 1886, allowing steam ships to berth alongside even at low water, and this stimulated a burst of building activity in the Mooragh area of the town, while in Peel a promenade and hotels were built in the 1880s, and also a fine new church, destined one day to be the cathedral of St German. The 1880s also saw a rapid expansion of Port Erin, again with a promenade bristling with hotels and boarding houses. Port St Mary developed less dramatically, while the rather snooty residents of Castletown turned their faces away from the 'visiting trade' almost completely, with the result that Derbyhaven remained undeveloped and the population of Castletown itself declined steadily.

Walpole's main achievement politically was a financial arrangement in 1890, later the basis of the 'Common Purse Scheme', which ensured that the Island was not disadvantaged by UK customs and tax regulations. In 1893 he published his *Land of Home Rule*, a history of the Island and its constitutional development. It included a description of his powers as Lieutenant Governor, which he conceded had become very great. After providing a long list of the Governor's responsibilities he noted that 'the Governor appears possessed of almost autocratic authority'. This was not welcome news to many Manx politicians who in any case considered that 'Home Rule' was a myth. In Tynwald the Manx had their own parliament, it was true, but through the Governor the UK exercised executive control. Walpole left in 1893 to run the UK's Post Office, to write more history books, and eventually gain a knighthood. He was succeeded by Sir West Ridgeway, a shooting star who achieved eminence in the Indian army and civil service before being appointed Under-Secretary for Ireland in 1889. He inherited from Walpole a Bill which set up local authorities called Commissioners, headed by a Chairman, and these remain today except in Douglas, which had a Mayor and Corporation after 1896. Ridgeway had hardly finished steering this legislation through Tynwald, however, when he left in 1895 on his appointment as Governor of Ceylon (now Sri Lanka).

It was during Ridgeway's short stay on the Island that the banker Alexander Bruce became a leading figure in the Isle of Man Tramways and Electric Power Company which was set up to harness the newly-discovered miracle of electricity. Between 1892 and 1894 the company constructed an electric tramway from the northern end of Douglas promenade along the coast to Laxey and in the next two years the line was taken to the top of Snaefell. At the same time a cable railway, similar to the ones built in San Francisco, took street trams up the steep incline of Prospect Hill in central Douglas. A separate company opened a line along a newly constructed 'Marine Drive' from Douglas to Port Soderick in 1897 and in 1898 the existing line to Laxey was extended all the way to Ramsey. These colourful trams following so scenic a route rapidly became a major tourist attraction as well as providing useful transport links, following in the tradition of the

171

The Snaefell Mine. (Manx National Heritage)

horse-drawn trams which had already been operating on Douglas promenade for several years.

Loch, Walpole and Ridgeway had all been exceptionally able and forward-looking administrators but Lord Henniker, appointed in 1895, was a courtier, country landowner and member of the House of Lords who had very little experience of government or financial administration. Moreover, he was very unlucky. In May 1897 twenty miners died in the Snaefell mine as a result of being poisoned by gas. Then in February 1900 Alexander Bruce, who had up to now been a hero on the Island, became one of its chief villains because Dumbell's Bank, of which he was the general manager and which was the biggest on the Island, collapsed, ruining many of its eight thousand depositors. Henniker was criticized for a dilatory approach to this crisis but he eventually presided over a trial which found Bruce and four other employees of the Bank guilty of financial misconduct. It was twenty years before creditors received back about two-thirds of their original deposits and many Manx families experienced great hardship. Henniker inevitably got some of the blame for all this and he was generally perceived to be somewhat lazy, often late for appointments and also incompetent because on two occasions during his time administrative blunders resulted in there being no new laws to be read out on Tynwald Day for official promulgation.

The collapse of Dumbell's Bank was not the only economic difficulty the Island faced by the turn of the century. Manx agriculture did not suffer from the depression which hit the UK in the 1870s, largely because of the needs of the visiting trade, and indeed in 1900 it was generally considered that Manx farmers were among the most prosperous in the British Isles, though most of the upland crofts were abandoned between 1885 and 1900. The fishing industry picked itself up from the doldrums of the 1850s, partly because Robert Corrin of Peel pioneered the fishing of mackerel off Kinsale, in Ireland, from 1861 onwards and other skippers sailed to the Shetlands in search of herring. By 1880 the number of Manx fishing boats had increased to 393, crewed by about 2,600 men and boys. By this time Manx boats had adapted some of the features of the successful Cornish luggers and known as 'nickeys' they were thought to be some of the best fishing boats afloat. Peel became the undisputed centre of this renewed activity and there was serious overcrowding in the harbour in 1880. Increasingly, many of the herrings were smoked in cure-houses in Peel to produce the Manx 'kippers' which still enjoy international fame.

Barrels of herrings at Peel. (Manx National Heritage)

Then from 1884 to1898 the shoals of herring, which had often been up to ten miles long and four miles wide, could no longer be found. Official inquiries failed to pinpoint the reasons and the results were that many young men, with no crofting left to fall back on, either went to work in the holiday industry or left the Island in search of work abroad. When the herring shoals returned to Manx waters between 1899 and 1914 the fishing fleet had become out of date and most fishermen were elderly. By 1913 the fleet was down to 185 vessels, crewed by only 677 individuals, and it declined steadily throughout the rest of the twentieth century.

The mining boom which the Island experienced from about 1830 to 1880 also began to quieten down. The five Foxdale and two Laxey mines employed over a thousand workers in the 1870s and 1880s, with lead the speciality at Foxdale and silver and zinc at Laxey. But the mines were not inexhaustible, there were difficulties with export facilities and above all there was serious competition from South Africa, Australia, the USA and Canada. When jobs began to dry up on the Island many Manx miners emigrated to these countries and established expatriate communities there. By 1900 only three mines were still working, one of them the Snaefell mine which was the scene of the 1897 disaster. It closed in 1905 and the last Foxdale mine followed it in 1911 while the last Laxey mine struggled on until 1929.

Queen Victoria died in January 1901 and Lord Henniker duly proclaimed her son Edward VII Lord of Man on Tynwald Hill. This prompted an interesting response from the Manx Attorney-General, Sir James Gell, whose view was that the new king's title ought to be 'King of Man and the Isles' given the fact that Man was an ancient kingdom despite the second Earl of Derby's decision to call himself 'Lord of Man' during the reign of Henry VIII. Even though Gell's opinion came from an influential and respected legal source, it made little impact at the time and has made little since. Late in June 1902 Henniker suddenly died, aged 58, and his coffin was shipped back to England for burial. In an obituary the *Isle of Man Advertiser* wrote frankly that 'with no very great aptitude for business details and little taste for parliamentary life, he did not shine as he might have done as President of the Tynwald Court and Head of the Executive in the Island.' Before his replacement arrived, the new King Edward VII and Queen Alexandra arrived in Douglas Bay on the Royal Yacht on August 24th 1902 and entertained many dignitaries on board that night. The following day the Royal Yacht sailed to Ramsey where the royal pair disembarked and drove first to Bishopscourt, then on to Peel for lunch, arriving in Douglas in the afternoon and travelling back to Ramsey on the electric tram. As Queen Victoria had not gone ashore on her visit in 1847 this was the first time a reigning British monarch had set foot on the Isle of Man.

Shortly after this, the new Lieutenant Governor, Lord Raglan, took up office in September. He was the grandson of the Crimean Field Marshal and after Eton and Sandhurst he served with the army in India and in the second Afghan War. In 1884 he succeeded to his father's title and estates in Monmouthshire and he sat in the House of Lords as a keen Tory supporter. In 1900 he was appointed to the important ministerial post of Under Secretary for War and played a significant part in planning the campaigns of the Boer War. He was aged 45 when he came to the Island, very tall and sporting an impressive 'handlebar' moustache. His wife was a daughter of the Earl of Bessborough and they had three sons and three daughters.

Lord and Lady Raglan presided over the Edwardian summer of the Isle of Man when in many ways it enjoyed boom conditions as a holiday destination, fortunately offsetting decline in the fishing and mining industries. The number of visitors each year increased steadily, reaching a record 634,512 in 1913, ferried across to the Island by the ships of the Steam Packet Company which were by now no less than

Edwardian Douglas. (Manx National Heritage)

seventeen in number. The promenades and beach of Douglas were thronged with thousands of people by day, while at night they could choose from a great array of entertainment venues, such as Frank Matcham's Gaiety Theatre or the Palace Ballroom, one of the largest dance halls in Europe, boasting 16,000 square feet of parquet flooring. A Tower had been contemplated, in ultimate defiance of Blackpool, but it was never built. Raglan was also a keen supporter of the 'Tourist Trophy' races for cars (1905) and motorcycles (1907) and encouraged Tynwald to allow closure of the necessary roads. The car races ended in 1922 but the TT races for touring bikes developed into the Island's most famous international sporting event. Also Henry Bloom Noble, a wealthy merchant who died childless in 1903, left nearly all his fortune for philanthropic purposes on the Island. Among the many results of this was the building of a new 'Noble's' hospital in Douglas and the demolition of his former home, the Villa Marina, to make way for the construction on its site of the 'Kursaal', a polygonal concert hall and ballroom opened by the Raglans in 1913.

Raglan was at his best in these circumstances because on social occasions he was invariably charming and very personable, but in politics he proved himself to be intractably conservative and stubborn. This was most unfortunate because in the wake of Henniker's poor performance there was a growing demand in Tynwald for reforms of the constitution and in particular a decrease in the powers of the Governor. In 1903 Samuel Norris, a radical journalist, founded the Manx National Reform League and after the accession to power of the Liberals in the UK in 1906 he hoped for some progress. In 1907 the Keys sent a petition to the Home Secretary demanding a wide range of changes including a fixed term of office for the Governor and an Executive Council to advise him. Raglan blocked negotiations at every opportunity and also refused to introduce social reforms on the Island such as old age pensions and better schooling. In 1911 the Keys went 'on strike' after Raglan had ruled that they were out of order and they only agreed to co-operate with him when a Commission under Lord MacDonnell was set up to inquire into their grievances about the constitution. MacDonnell's report of 1911 recommended a fixed term for the Governor and modifications to the Council, though Raglan energetically opposed all change. Eventually he was overruled by the Home Office but by then war had broken out and the reforms were shelved for the duration. Raglan certainly adhered closely to his family motto *I scorn to change or fear.*

Chapter Thirteen
The twentieth century

TWO WORLD WARS, 1914-1945

The outbreak of hostilities between Britain and Germany in August 1914 brought a sudden halt to the Isle of Man's summer holiday season because thirteen of the Steam Packet's ships were requisitioned and the threat of enemy submarines lurking in the Irish Sea put an end to regular services. As a result the tourist trade collapsed during the war years, bringing serious hardship to hotel and boarding house keepers, whose livelihood was ruined. Douglas became something of a ghost town, its splendid new Villa Marina unused and empty. The UK, with scant reference to Tynwald, decided that the Island was ideal for interning 'enemy aliens', who were Germans, Austrians and other 'enemies' who happened to be in the UK when war was declared. A large camp, eventually accommodating over 20,000 people, (more than the population of Douglas) was set up at Knockaloe, near Peel, and its organization and administration was largely undertaken by Lord Raglan, with notable success. The provisioning and servicing of such a large number of detainees brought prosperous trade to many farmers and business people on the Island, though that was no consolation to the hoteliers. Raglan also called up three companies of Manx volunteers who later served with the British army in Salonika: altogether some 8,000 Manxmen fought in this war.

In December 1915 Samuel Norris founded the 'Isle of Man War Rights Union' with the object of persuading the Manx government to reduce rates on business premises in order to help the Douglas hoteliers. In June 1916, with no progress made, a mass meeting called for Raglan's resignation and on Tynwald Day in July hundreds of people wore badges stamped with the letters RMG, for 'Raglan Must Go', and someone, (probably a mischievous boy) threw a clump of grass at the Governor. It missed, but the incident was widely and sensationally reported in Manx and UK papers. The reformers' case was taken up by *The Manchester Guardian*, and Norris sent a petition to Parliament calling for Raglan's replacement. Meanwhile an auction was held on the Island of property which had been seized from those

Racing on the St John's Course used from 1907 to 1910. (FotoFinders)

who had not paid their rates and Norris persuaded some 600 people at the auction not to make bids. For this he was hauled before a Court chaired by Raglan and required to apologize, and when he refused he was sent to prison, where he remained for twenty-eight days.

Raglan had won this round but then owing largely to circumstances beyond his control he was forced to announce in 1917 that in order to pay for subsidized bread, income tax would be introduced on the Island - a measure that was deeply unpopular with Tynwald, many of whose members were very prosperous. So they refused the necessary legislation, the price of bread rocketed, and on July 4th 1918 there was a general strike on the Island and Raglan had to cancel Tynwald Day. He went to London to discuss the crisis with the Home Office and came back with instructions to tell Tynwald that if they did not sanction income tax within two weeks, it would be imposed upon the Island by Parliament. Faced with this, Tynwald, having prevaricated until the last possible day, gave in. The war came to an end in November and Raglan announced his resignation the following month. He was 61 years old and had suffered several bouts of serious ill-health, no doubt made worse by stress, and he died in 1921.

After Raglan the Home Office realized that they needed someone on the Island who would appease the demand for constitutional

Lord Raglan. (Manx National Heritage)

reform, and the man chosen was Major-General William Fry, whose wife was a daughter of John Goldie-Taubman, owner of the Nunnery estate in Douglas. As recommended by the MacDonnell commission Fry was appointed for a limited tenure of seven years and the membership of the Council was significantly modified. The archdeacon, vicar general and receiver general lost their seats and the new eleven-member Council, now generally called the 'Legislative Council', consisted of the Governor, the bishop, the two deemsters, the attorney general, two members nominated by the Governor and four elected by the Keys. Fry encouraged Tynwald to introduce old age pensions and an improved education system and did his best to sort out some difficult issues left over from the Raglan years concerning the salaries of public servants, the Island's contribution to the cost of the war, and the level of rates. He also sanctioned payment of MHKs for the first time (£50 a year plus travelling expenses). When Fry left in 1926 it was with popular approval and the presention of a fine silver casket.

The Steam Packet's requisitioned ships had suffered heavily in the war - only three survived - but new ones were commissioned and others were chartered and in 1919 343,332 visitors arrived, rising to 561,124 in 1920. There was then a dip during the 1920s because of the economic depression in the UK, followed by a steady rise in the 1930s to 585,508 in 1939. The holidaymakers came from much the same locations as before the war and a very popular destination was Cunningham's Holiday Camp in Douglas which provided tented and chalet accommodation for up to 4,000 young men who were fed in a dining-hall seating 3,000. Between the wars over a million young men enjoyed these facilities despite the strict regulations concerning behaviour and dress. A colonnade and arcade were added to the Villa Marina in 1930 and 1931 and the Loch promenade was widened and the sunken Marine Gardens built between 1929 and 1935 - causing much disruption. This was the age of the cinema, with films being shown at the Picture House, the Royalty, the Regal and the impressive white 'art deco' Crescent cinema built in 1930.

By then the Lieutenant Governor was Sir Claude Hill (1926-1933) who had been a high-ranking Indian civil servant and Director-General of the Red Cross. He proved to be an efficient and conscientious administrator and managed to solve the vexed question of the Island's contribution to the expense of the war. He also set up an experimental four-man Tynwald 'Consultative Committee' to advise him. This came to his rescue in 1931 when he disagreed with the Keys over the need to supply public electricity. They persuaded him to change his mind and he and his wife opened the Pulrose power station in 1933. He was a great supporter of the TT and was largely behind the first government grant to the races in 1929, intended to encourage foreign competitors. The Hills were an elegant and popular couple and they acquired two fine Parisian chandeliers which still grace Government House. Unfortunately Hill was not in the best of health and he died in 1934, only a few months after he left the Island. He was succeeded for a short time by Sir Montagu Butler, who had been Governor of the vast Central Provinces of India. His period in office coincided with the completion of a major extension to Douglas Harbour which was opened in 1936 and named the 'King Edward VIII Pier' in honour of the new King, who soon abdicated in favour of his brother George VI.

It was fortunate that the holiday trade was able to re-establish itself after the war because in most other respects the economic position on the Island was not good. The population reached about 60,000 in 1921 but fell by ten thousand over the next decade as many left in search of work. Mining had come to an end, agriculture suffered badly from foreign competition and there were only 57 fishing vessels at sea in 1914, falling to 47 in 1937 with crews numbering only 128. This was not caused by a lack of herring but by competition from fishing fleets from Lowestoft, Yarmouth and the Moray Firth. In 1937 Manx boats began dredging for scallops, which developed into a more profitable trade. Nor was there much investment in technology or manufacture in the 1920s and 1930s with the important exception of motor transport. From 1919 the motorcycle TT races, suspended during the war, again became an annual feature of Island life and brought it international fame arguably for the first time in its history. In addition the Manx Motor Club organized in 1923 what are now the Manx Grand Prix races for amateur riders. The Glencrutchery Road grandstand was constructed in 1926 and the entertainment star George Formby's film *No Limit,* with a storyline based on the TT races, reached a wide audience in Britain and abroad. During the 1930s the dominance of British bikes was challenged by Italian and German machines. In 1939 BMW were among the winners and their bikes with a sidecar equipped with a machine gun became a well-known feature of the coming war. Throughout the 1920s and 1930s Tynwald spent more on highway improvement than on anything else and Douglas Corporation established an ever-growing fleet of motor buses.

Sir Montagu Butler left in 1937 to become Master of Pembroke College, Cambridge, and possibly with the security of the Island in mind at a time when war with Nazi Germany was a distinct possibility, the Home Office appointed Vice-Admiral Leveson-Gower (soon Earl Granville) to succeed him. Granville and his wife brought a touch of semi-regal aura to Government House because Lady

'King Orry' (3), eventually lost at Dunkirk. (Ferry Publications Library)

Granville was a sister of Queen Elizabeth, consort of George VI. One of the new Governor's first acts was to frame a bill in 1937 which committed Tynwald to paying £100,000 a year to the cost of rearmament in the UK in return for which the Air Ministry would construct a new grass airfield on a 300-acre site at Jurby. There were protests from local farmers but the airfield brought a population of three to four hundred to the north of the Island and benefited service industries accordingly. RAF Jurby opened in September 1939, just

after war was declared against Germany, and tarmac runways were completed in 1942. The airfield was mostly used for the training of navigation, bomb-aiming and air-gunnery and by 1944 up to eighty Avro Anson trainers were based there, though unfortunately their accident rate in training flights was very high, with 250 recorded crashes on the Island and more than 200 air crew killed.

From October 1940 German bombers began night attacks on British cities using airfields in northern France, which put Belfast, Glasgow and Liverpool well within range, and the Air Ministry decided it needed a fighter station on the Island. About 500 acres of land were requisitioned from local farmers round Andreas and a triangle of three intersecting runways was constructed by local labour and Irish navvies. The airfield became operational as a base for Spitfire fighters in the spring of 1942, though in 1943 it became an Air Gunnery School. In 1943 the Admiralty informed the Manx Government that it intended to develop the existing Ronaldsway airfield into a Royal Navy station of 850 acres as a training centre for the new Fairey Barracuda torpedo/dive bombers which were likely to be used against the Japanese in the South Pacific. Over 500 men constructed the four runways, control tower and outbuildings, which involved the demolition of the historic Ronaldsway farmhouse and the disruption of an important archaeological site. Named HMS *Urley* the new station was commissioned in June 1944 and by January 1945 there were three squadrons based there, flying between sixty and seventy aircraft a day.

When hostilities began in September 1939 Granville set up a 'War Cabinet' consisting of two members of the Legislative Council and five members of the Keys, which would meet once a week and deliberate in secret. As with the first war, the tourist trade came to a sudden halt and ten of the Steam Packet's 16 ships were requisitioned and eight became heroes of the evacuation from Dunkirk in 1940, carrying some 24,669 troops to safety between them, though the *King Orry*, which had proudly led the German fleet to surrender in Scapa Flow in 1918, was one of three Steam Packet ships to be sunk in one day, the 29th of May. Also as before, enemy aliens were interned on the Island though this time lessons were learnt and they were accommodated chiefly in the empty hotels and boarding houses in Douglas, Ramsey and Peel. In Douglas there were six camps, Granville on the Loch Promenade for about 750 men, Sefton round the Sefton Hotel for about 600, Metropole - mainly for some 500

Italians, Palace with nearly 3,000 detainees in and around the Palace Hotel, Central with 2,000 detainees in 34 houses behind the Central Promenade, and Hutchinson Camp in Hutchinson Square where the musicians who subsequently became the world-famous Amadeus string quartet were held. The camps were all surrounded with barbed wire fences and access was closely supervised.

In Onchan about 60 houses around Royal Avenue were fenced off and in Peel the Peveril Camp was established at the northern end of the promenade. In Ramsey Mooragh Camp, the first Island camp to open, in May 1940, was created by requisitioning the hotels along the promenade in front of Mooragh Park and it held Germans, Finns and Italians until it closed in 1945. All these camps were for men. A small number of women and children were held in Rushen Camp which was effectively the whole of the south peninsula, cut off by a barbed wire fence stretching from Fleshwick to Gansey and including Port Erin and Port St Mary. Internees were billeted on local residents who were paid one pound one shilling a week. Some married couples were allowed to live together at a camp on Bradda Head. Whereas the internees of the 1914-18 war had all been loyal to their nations of origin, most of the Germans and Austrians held in the Isle of Man between 1940 and 1945 were in fact refugees from the Nazi regime who had sought asylum in Britain and most were released within eighteen months. The greatest number of internees was held during 1940 and 1941, after which several of the camps closed.

As it was considered to be a relatively safe location, Douglas became the home of air bases and training schools for gunnery and radar and several thousand young servicemen and women kept the town a busy and even cheerful place during the war, while the presence of the thousands of internees meant that the shopkeepers and suppliers carried on a profitable trade. Cunningham's former Holiday Camp became HMS *St George* which trained 8,677 boy seamen in conditions of rigorous discipline between 1939 and 1945 while the Villiers Hotel was used as an Officer Cadet Training Unit. The Majestic Hotel on Onchan Head was converted into a hospital run by the Royal Army Medical Corps and the Douglas Head Hotel produced thirty thousand radar operators in its new role as the radar training school HMS *Valkyrie*. Tynwald accepted the UK legislation of 1939 which conscripted men up to the age of 41, but in an interesting show of independence refused to extend it to 51 when the UK did so two years later. Perhaps by way of response the UK extended

Granville's seven year tenure by one year (because of the war), without reference to Tynwald. With three airfields, many training schools, its internment camps and the requisitioned ships of the Steam Packet, the Isle of Man can claim to have played a significant part in the war effort. Most of all, some 5,455 Manxmen served in the British forces or Merchant Navy during the war and 490 lost their lives.

TOWARDS EFFECTIVE SELF-GOVERNMENT 1945-1980

Air Vice-Marshal Sir Geoffrey Bromet was chosen to succeed Granville, who left in September 1945 to become Governor of Northern Ireland. Perhaps mindful of the Island's contribution to the war Attlee's Labour Government authorized Bromet to accept Tynwald's long-standing demands for a permanent Executive Council, consisting of seven senior members of Tynwald, which was set up in October 1946. The Council was chaired by Bromet and met once a week to discuss major policy decisions. The Home Office also promised in 1949 that it would allow at some point in the future a major transfer of control over expenditure to Tynwald. In 1950 Tynwald contested Bromet's Budget proposals and income tax increases and also financial decisions he made in the following year. The Keys then produced a 'Home Rule Charter' with eight demands which were sent to the Home Secretary but the Labour Government fell and the issue was sidelined.

Meanwhile the Island got back into its stride as a holiday resort, especially after the purchase from the Admiralty in 1947 of Ronaldsway aerodrome, on which over £2 million had been spent during the war. Air transport had started tentatively in the 1920s with the first commercial flight consisting of a light aeroplane carrying copies of a motorcycle magazine, which landed on Douglas Head in 1925. In 1928 a three-engined aircraft, carrying the same magazines, used a 68-acre field at Ronaldsway farm near Castletown. British Amphibious Airlines began the first passenger service in 1932, flying from Blackpool with four passengers a time. By 1934 other companies carried a total of 5,095 passengers from Ronaldsway during the year, rising to 21,200 in 1939. By 1949 the figure reached over 41,000. However, most visitors still came by boat. The Steam Packet lost four ships at Dunkirk but they were replaced with new ones and in 1949 there were over 570,000 arrivals by sea.

From 1947 onwards Joe Loss and his band played at the Villa Marina and made it famous throughout the UK with his BBC broadcasts but it became clear by the early 1950s that the Island's economic revival had run into problems. The average number of visitors a year between 1950 and 1960 was only 520,000, a drop of 17% on pre-war figures, caused probably by the expense of travel to the Island and the somewhat outdated facilities now on offer. Also the fishing industry collapsed, with only 70 fishermen and 24 boats operating by the early 1960s. During the winter months about 2,000 people were unemployed and the natural response was for Manx people to leave the Island in search of work. Accordingly the Island's population, which had recovered somewhat during the 1930s and 1940s, fell again from 55,253 in 1951 down to 48,135 in 1961. A new generation of Manx politicians, led by Charles Kerruish, a young northern farmer with exceptional political and debating skills, was firmly of the opinion that the Island would not recover from these difficulties while it was under the semi-colonial control of the UK and it was his ambition as an MHK, as well as that of Clifford Irving and Victor Kneale, among others in Tynwald, to achieve a far greater measure of self-government for the Island.

Under Sir Ambrose Dundas (1952-1959), who had been Governor of India's North West Frontier Province, the reformers made a good deal of progress. Prolonged negotiations took place with the Home Office about the handover of financial control and these culminated in a formal agreement signed in 1957 by which the Acts of 1866 and 1867 were repealed so that the UK handed over to Tynwald control of the Manx customs revenues, finance, police, loans, civil service and harbours. In fact this made the workload of the Governor, who was still Tynwald's chief executive, even greater, so the next step demanded by the reformers was a reduction in his powers. In 1958, the year before he left the Island, Dundas was persuaded to set up a five-man commission under Lord MacDermott to inquire into the constitution and make recommendations for reform.

Dundas was succeeded by Sir Ronald Garvey (1959-1966), who had been Governor of British Honduras (now Belize) and Fiji. Under him important recommendations of the MacDermott report were put into effect and in 1961 the powers of the Executive Council were greatly increased, so that the Governor would seldom be able to reject its advice. Moreover a Finance Board was created which would advise the Governor on all financial matters and his control over the civil service and police was limited. In the Legislative Council the second deemster lost his seat and the number of elected members was increased from four to five. As a result of these measures the Governor remained powerful, but subject to considerable restraints.

Garvey, who got on very well with Charles Kerruish who was by now Speaker of the House of Keys, threw himself with enthusiasm into the task of reviving the Isle of Man's economy. Dundas had done a good deal to set up new manufacturing and light engineering businesses and these initiatives were continued. However, Garvey felt that more could be done than this. His main idea was to attract wealthy residents to the Island, reducing tax levels at a time when UK income tax was exceptionally high. In 1960 surtax was abolished on the Island and income tax was pegged at a maximum of 22.5 per

Sir Charles Kerruish

cent, spectacularly lower than the UK. Garvey also pursued the controversial idea of establishing a casino, which eventually opened in 1966. In addition, he was a great supporter of the project to establish a commercial radio station on the Island, which, like the popular 'Radio Luxembourg', would reach across the UK and into Europe, thus raising the profile of the Island internationally. Tynwald authorized Manx Radio broadcasts from 7th June 1964 but the UK infuriated Manx politicians by refusing to allow the new station to broadcast outside the boundaries of the Island. To get its own back Tynwald turned a blind eye when the pirate radio ship 'Radio Caroline' dropped anchor off Ramsey Bay in July 1964 and began transmitting on British airwaves.

Garvey was succeeded by Sir Peter Stallard (1966-1973) who had also been Governor of British Honduras. Shortly after his arrival Tynwald voted to remove his power of appointing two members of the Executive Council and he was also soon embroiled in a major row between Tynwald and Harold Wilson's Labour Government over Radio Caroline. In 1965 the UK signed up to an international treaty outlawing pirate radio stations and expected Tynwald to follow suit. When Tynwald refused to introduce the necessary legislation the UK extended its Broadcasting (Offences) Act to the Island by Order in Council in 1967, to the fury of Charles Kerruish and many others. This row received a good deal of international press coverage and it seemed to many political observers that the Isle of Man had become a rebel second only to Ian Smith's Rhodesia. When in 1968 the UK set up the Kilbrandon commission to inquire into the British Government's relationship with Scotland and Wales, it also included the Isle of Man and the Channel Isles, in the hope that disagreements could be smoothed out.

In 1970 the Wilson Government fell, to be replaced by the Tories under Edward Heath, who successfully negotiated the UK's entry to the European 'Common Market'. This was a major worry for the Island's politicians and Charles Kerruish led a number of delegations to discuss the position with the Home Office which formally suggested that complete independence for the Island was an option acceptable to the UK. But members of Tynwald were not prepared to go that far at this stage and Kerruish was delighted with the eventual outcome - Protocol Three to the Treaty of Accession, by which the Island did not become a member of the Common Market but enjoyed many of its benefits.

Stallard's last months in office were overshadowed by the tragic fire in August 1973 at 'Summerland', a recently-opened leisure complex at the Onchan end of Douglas Bay. The fire resulted in the deaths of at least fifty people, with many more injured, and it naturally received extensive international media coverage. Once Stallard had gone there was yet another row when it was discovered that the wife of his designated successor would not be accompanying her husband to Government House. The Island's press railed against this decision and the Governor-designate resigned. The Home Office then found a 'safe pair of hands' in the person of Sir John Paul, who had been Governor of The Gambia, British Honduras and the Bahamas. In his time there, The Gambia and the Bahamas were granted independence, so he came to the Isle of Man quite prepared for major constitutional concessions.

To start with, in response to Tynwald's demands, he was appointed for only five years instead of seven. Moreover, the Kilbrandon Commission, in its report of 1973, while asserting that Parliament had the ultimate power to legislate for the Isle of Man on all matters, formally accepted the convention that Parliament does not legislate for the Island on domestic matters without the consent of Tynwald. This was considered an important concession on the Island and it led the way for major reductions in the powers of the Governor. In 1976 financial policy became the responsibility of the Finance Board and not the Governor, and an Act of 1980 declared that in future the Governor should no longer preside over or attend meetings of the Legislative Council or chair the Executive Council. A great many other powers of the Governor were distributed among the relevant Government Boards, so that Charles Kerruish was able to claim (not entirely correctly) that at last the Governor's authority had become 'a rubber stamp'.

This was a good time to advertise widely the great antiquity of Tynwald, and Kerruish was a strong supporter of the notion that 1979 should be celebrated as its Millennium Year. Although the specific chronology was shaky, it could be claimed that as a law-making institution Tynwald reached back at least a thousand years, making the UK parliament look a youngster by comparison. Sir John and Lady Paul, who were very popular on the Island, were asked to stay an extra year in order to preside over the elaborate celebrations which included visits from Queen Elizabeth II, the King of Norway, Princess Margaretha of Sweden, the Presidents of Iceland and Malta, the US Ambassador to the UK, the Lord Mayor of London and many others. It was a suitable way to celebrate the Island's achievement of effective self-government.

MINISTERIAL GOVERNMENT AND THE RISE OF THE FINANCE SECTOR

As laid down by the recent legislation, Rear-Admiral Sir Nigel Cecil (1980-1985) did not preside over or attend meetings of the Legislative Council and did not chair the Executive Council, though he still presided over full meetings of Tynwald. The political initiative passed mainly to the members of the Executive Council and its Chairmen, who were Percy Radcliffe (1981-1985) and Dr Edgar Mann (1985-1986). In 1986 the existing government boards were converted into nine departments, each headed by a minister, and the post of Chief Minister was created, held first by (Sir) Miles Walker (1986-1996) then Donald Gelling (1996-2001), Richard Corkill (2001-2004) and Donald Gelling again (2004-2006), followed by Tony Brown in 2006. In 1989 the Executive Council was renamed the Council of Ministers and it was decided that after 1990 the Governor would no longer preside over Tynwald. A new post of President of Tynwald was created with Sir Charles Kerruish elected as its first holder (1990-2000), followed by Noel Cringle. The President's role is to chair meetings of the Legislative Council, the 'upper house' of Tynwald, consisting of eight members elected by the House of Keys for a period of four years, as well as the Bishop and the non-voting Attorney General, and then to preside over full meetings of Tynwald which consist of both the Legislative Council and the 24 members of the House of Keys. This meant that the subsequent Lieutenant Governors had very little political role to play, though they carried out many other responsibilities and social duties as the Sovereign's representative.

It is therefore the case that since 1980 the Island has effectively been governed by Manx politicians within a ministerial system. The Chief Minister, once elected by Tynwald, appoints and dismisses his ministers as he thinks fit and policy is largely formulated in the Council of Ministers and then subjected to the scrutiny of Tynwald. The one-party system has generally been maintained though short-lived opposition groups have come and gone. The great advantage of the ministerial system is that it enables the Manx Government to react more effectively and immediately to the needs of the Island and

191

to represent its interests internationally. Critics of the Manx system argue that because there is no official political opposition, government policy and practice are not subject to satisfactory scrutiny. The system of election to the House of Keys has been modified over the years to take account of population growth, especially in Douglas and Onchan. By the general election of 2006 Douglas had been divided into four electoral districts, (North, South, East and West) with two members each, and Onchan and Rushen had three members each. Ramsey had two members and Ayre, Castletown, Garff, Glenfaba, Malew and Santon, Middle, Michael and Peel had one member each. For the election of 2006 the voting age was lowered from 18 to 16 to encourage the participation of young people in the political system.

The Summerland fire resulted in a raft of fire regulations which proved too expensive for many hotels and boarding houses already operating on the borderline, and their number fell drastically from 1,142 to 620 between 1970 and 1980. Unexpectedly, the number of visitors coming to the Island increased in the same decade, averaging 527,000 compared with 474,000 in the 1960s. This was partly because of increased fuel costs, which made international package holidays more expensive. During the 1980s tourism on the Island went into marked decline as package holidays became cheap again, the cost of travel to the Island seemed high and the quality of accommodation low. The proportion of the Manx national income provided by tourism fell from eleven per cent in 1983 to six per cent in 1995, agriculture and fishing provided only between two and three per cent and even manufacturing declined from 15 to 11 per cent. Some of Douglas' most iconic hotels, such as the Villiers, the Douglas Head and the Majestic, closed down and were eventually demolished.

Fortunately the main positive development in the 1970s was the rise of the finance industry on the Island, which by 1983 provided 21 per cent of the national income. In 1972 the sterling area was limited to Britain, the Channel Islands, Eire and the Isle of Man and in 1979 exchange controls in Britain were suspended, which brought a halt to the Bank of England's control over offshore financial centres in the British Isles. As a result a considerable number of merchant banks established branches on the Island and this helped to increase the resident population from 54,581 in 1971 to 66,101 in 1981. There was a major problem in 1982 with the collapse of the Savings and Investment Bank, based on the Island, which had debts of £42

The 'Lady Isabella', Laxey. (Miles Cowsill)

million. This led the Manx Government to set up a Financial Supervision Commission in 1983 to license banks and impose regulations aimed at preventing corruption, malpractice and money-laundering and since then it has been the Manx Government's policy to conform with the increasing international demands for financial transparency.

Between 1981 and 1986 Tynwald passed a number of Acts which attracted insurance companies to the Island with financial incentives based on tax exemptions. Ten major companies were established by 1994, employing a thousand people, and between 1986 and 1991 there was also a rapid growth of 'captive' insurance companies, whose role was to insure the risks of their parent companies, and there were 130 of these on the Island by 1994. They held funds estimated at £2 billion, which in turn stimulated the growth of investment management companies. In 1986 the UKs Building Societies Act removed many restrictions from their operation and made the establishment of branches on the Isle of Man attractive for mortgages and deposits. Tynwald's Merchant Shipping Act of 1984 capitalized on the extension of international shipping conventions to the Isle of Man and encouraged ship-management companies to establish themselves on the Island, increasing from eight in 1986 to 23 in 1994. In 1986 a Freeport was constructed near Ronaldsway to provide a duty-free zone for items awaiting export.

In 1997 the Isle of Man Film and Television Fund was set up to encourage the film industry on the Island, and a studio complex was built in Lezayre. An Electronic Transactions Act in 2000 encouraged the development of e-commerce and information technology to keep the Island at the forefront of this rapidly-developing industry. Manx Telecom established itself as a leader in communications and satellite technology, and the Island was used as a testbed for the third generation of mobile phones. Tynwald also gave much financial support to traditional manufacturing ventures on the Island during this period. In 2004/5 the finance sector generated the greatest percentage of income for the Manx Treasury (35%), followed by professional and scientific services (18%) and other services (17%). Manufacturing and construction provided 8% each, with the tourist industry contributing only 6% and Public Administration 4%. The growth area of Information and Communications Technology (ICT) provided 3% with agriculture and fisheries a mere 1%.

The result of all this activity was that the Island's economy

Andreas Church. (Miles Cowsill)

prospered greatly and between 1986 and 2006 the resident population increased from 64,679 to about 79,000, just under half being Manx-born. This influx was the result of the creation of many well-paid posts in the finance sector and also of the attractiveness of a tax structure without inheritance or capital gains taxes and a top rate of 18% income tax (capped at £100,000 a year in 2006). VAT has been retained, and by 2007 it was the source of about 70% of the Island's income. Between 1961 and 1991 the towns grew steadily but the most dramatic increase was in Onchan, which ballooned from 3,618 in 1961 to 8,656 in 1996. Many 'luxury' houses and apartments were built on and around Onchan Head, the most spectacular being the redevelopment of the Majestic Hotel site in the early 2000s. In Douglas many of the Victorian boarding house terraces on the promenades were demolished and replaced by modern blocks of flats, while the Government, rich with the revenue that flowed from the success of the finance sector, embarked on many ambitious public sector building projects. These included new power stations in Douglas (1989) and Peel (1995), the National Sports Centre (from 1991) new Courts of Justice (1997), a sculpturally shaped incinerator (2004), a new Noble's Hospital on an extensive country site in Braddan (2004) and many new government office buildings in Douglas. Tynwald was also generous in its sponsorship of Manx National Heritage which had become responsible for most of the Island's places of scenic beauty and historic interest. Given all this, it can be argued that the three decades following 1980 have been the most prosperous in the Island's long history, outstripping even the dynamic development of the Island as a holiday resort in the late nineteenth century.

Chapter Fourteen
Contemporary Aspects

During the eighteenth century Manx Gaelic was still the language spoken by the vast majority of Manx people and there was little Manx literature as such. The main cultural tradition consisted of folklore passed down orally from generation to generation and this tended to be dominated by tales of supernatural creatures who had their origins far back in ancient myths and legends. Manannan mac Lir had pride of place and rushes are still strewn as a tribute to him on Tynwald Day as they have been at midsummer for centuries. The presence of the fairy folk was acknowledged by most tales and the 'little people' had to be appeased and cajoled to keep them in a benevolent mood. The hairy and naked 'Phynnodderee' was generally helpful, if not too clever, but the goblin-like Glashtin could be dangerous while the Buggane, who tore down church roofs, was definitely evil and the Moddey Dhoo, a phantom black dog roaming Peel Castle, was to be avoided at all costs. Even today

Ramsey harbour. (Miles Cowsill)

The ruined cathedral of St German, Peel. (Miles Cowsill)

many people are not prepared to cross the 'fairy bridge' on the main road to Ballasalla without mouthing a greeting to the fairies.

By 1800 the diocese of Sodor and Man had ceased to enforce many of the disciplinary and administrative powers that Bishop Wilson had sought to maintain, and indeed the bishopric itself came under threat on two occasions in the nineteenth century. In 1836 the UK Parliament highhandedly passed an Act which incorporated the bishopric within the diocese of Carlisle but this aroused so much anger and opposition on the Island that it was soon repealed. A plan to dismantle the diocese and include it within that of Liverpool was, as we have seen, seriously considered in 1875 but again abandoned in the face of strong protest. Since then the diocese has maintained its established position on the Island and successive bishops have, by virtue of their office, been important contributors to the legislative process as members of the upper chamber of Tynwald.

During the 1880s money was collected for the restoration of the ancient cathedral of St German but after much debate it was agreed that it would be better to spend it on the building of a new parish church in Peel, which was completed in 1884. Originally it had a tall spire which was severely damaged by a storm in 1907 and subsequently dismantled. The restoration of the old cathedral was often debated but no action was taken and the Bishop's chapel at Bishopscourt was used as a pro-cathedral in the meantime. In 1979, largely because the recently-appointed bishop, Vernon Nicholls, was reluctant to live in Bishopscourt because of its size and inconvenience, the historic house was controversially sold to a private individual and the decision was taken to consecrate the 1884 church in Peel as the Cathedral of St German in October 1980. The official residence of the bishop is currently a modern house on the outskirts of Douglas.

The Island's Ecclesiastical Census of 1851 gave a good picture of the relative strengths of the Anglican and Methodist communities, with the Anglicans maintaining 32 places of worship, Wesleyan Methodists 53, Primitive Methodists (established by John Butcher, a preacher from Bolton, in 1823) 23, Roman Catholics 4, Presbyterians 2 and Independents 2. By 1862 the Nonconformists had progressed further, with 91 chapels, 20 ministers and 200 local preachers. In 1850 the Roman Catholic Church hierarchy was re-established in Britain, the Island became part of the Liverpool diocese and in 1859 a fine Roman Catholic Church, St Mary's of the Isle, was opened in Douglas. There were stirrings of sectarian rivalry on the Island as the Protestant community faced up to the expansion of Roman Catholicism, but no serious conflict occurred. The numbers of Roman Catholics grew with the influx of workers from Ireland and Liverpool and churches were subsequently built in Ramsey, Peel, Port Erin, Pulrose and Onchan. As the Island developed into a major tourist resort the Nonconformist community objected to the mass consumption of alcohol and the Douglas Temperance Asssociation was inaugurated in 1894. During the twentieth century the most notable feature of the religious situation on the Island was that, for the most part, Anglicans and Nonconformists worked together in considerable harmony. Towards the end of the century a marked decline became apparent in the number of people attending religious services regularly and there was pressure to close places of worship or convert them to other uses.

Bishop Hildesley's success in having the Book of Common Prayer and the Bible translated into Manx Gaelic and published between 1763 and 1772 gave the language more stability and authority and a Manx dictionary was published in 1835 by Archibald Cregeen. Despite these advances, however, English steadily became the dominant language during the nineteenth century because Manx

MER at Onchan. (Miles Cowsill)

Gaelic was considered barbaric by preachers and educationalists, who urged the study of English. By the 1890s it was clear that Manx Gaelic would soon die out and this stimulated a flurry of activity among historians and antiquaries anxious to preserve records of it, chief among whom was Arthur W.Moore, a member of a distinguished Manx family. Educated at Rugby and Cambridge he became an MHK and eventually Speaker but also wrote a number of scholarly books about the Island, including ones on Manx carvals (1891), ballads and music (1896) and folklore. In 1900 he also published a very authoritative two-volume history of the Isle of Man which, while now inevitably out of date in some respects, is still invaluable as a work of reference.

The Gaelic Manx Society was inaugurated in 1899 and with its motto of 'Gyn chengey, gyn cheer' (without tongue, without country) it set about the preservation of the Manx language, especially under the vigorous influence after 1918 of its secretary Mona Douglas (1898 -1987), who devoted her life to the furtherance of many aspects of Manx culture. The Manx Youth Movement, founded in 1931, also dedicated itself to the teaching of Manx Gaelic and in 1964 'Mec Vannin' (the sons of Man) was founded to promote Manx nationalism in all its forms, including political independence. Enthusiasm for the Manx language has grown steadily and it has been estimated in 2007 that about 80 individuals have learnt to speak and write it fluently, with many hundreds more having studied it to a basic standard. A Gaelic play group movement gathered momentum in the 1990s and a Gaelic language school opened in St John's in 2002.

The Manx Museum, set up in 1922 under its first director, Philip Kermode, steadily became under his successors the main centre for the display of Manx historical exhibits and an important repository of documents and archives. By the 1980s it was the heart of 'Manx National Heritage', an organization charged by the Manx Government to protect, present and promote all aspects of Manx natural and cultural heritage both within and outside the Island. MNH is responsible for over 200 scheduled ancient monuments on the Island and over 2,000 acres of countryside and 22 properties. These include the impressive House of Manannan at Peel, an award-winning museum opened in 1995, and several other famous Island sites such as the two castles and the Laxey Wheel.

Scholarly study of the Island's archaeology, culture and history has been enormously advanced since the opening in Douglas in 1992 of the University of Liverpool's Centre for Manx Studies which has

Harry Kelly's Cottage at Cregneash, one of Manx National Heritage's main attractions. (DOT&L)

The statue of T.E.Brown in Douglas. (Miles Cowsill)

offered MA and D.Phil courses in Manx history, sponsored many lectures by visiting academics and in particular promoted a five-volume scholarly history of the Island to replace that published by A.W. Moore in 1900. The Manx Heritage Foundation was set up by Tynwald in 1982 to promote and support all aspects of Manx culture and together with an active group of Island publishers it has in recent years supported a remarkably large number of books about the Island. The Isle of Man College, established in 1976, provides further education opportunities in a wide range of disciplines and the Isle of Man Business School, opened in 1999, offers courses leading to the degree of Master of Business Administration. It occupies the splendid former mansion house known as 'The Nunnery', built close to the site of the old priory in Douglas. The only backward step in the academic area in recent times has been the closure in 2006 of Liverpool University's Port Erin Marine Laboratory which after its opening in 1892 gradually gained international recognition in its field. The Island's five state secondary schools are co-educational and the Island and Anglesey were the first parts of the British Isles to organize their schools on comprehensive lines, as early as 1946. As yet there is no Manx university and the Government subsidizes Manx students at British and other universities.

The Island's most distinguished literary figure is Thomas Edward Brown (1830-1897), a son of the Vicar of Braddan, who was educated at King William's College and Oxford where he was elected a fellow of Oriel College. He became Vice-Principal of King William's, a headmaster in Gloucester and Second Master of Clifton College in Bristol but alongside his career as a schoolmaster he was a productive poet whose best work is a series of poems in Manx dialect known as the *Fo'c'sle Yarns* depicting Manx life among the fishermen, miners and country folk of the mid-nineteenth century. His characterization of the Manx and acute observation of their moods, strengths and weaknesses did much to create a sense of national identity and he was formally proclaimed the Manx National Poet in 1930, the centenary of his birth. Brown also wrote poems in standard English which were published in a complete edition of his work by Macmillan and he was a profuse writer of stylish and scholarly letters. In 1911 the World Manx Association was formed, largely to promote the memory and the patriotic ideals of Brown and it has developed into an organization with many branches in the UK, Australia, the USA, New Zealand, Canada, South Africa and elsewhere.

Brown did all he could to encourage other Manx writers, in particular Thomas Henry Hall Caine who achieved phenomenal sales of his romantic novels, seven of which were based on the Island. Translated into all European languages, Hall Caine was famous in his lifetime (1853-1931) as 'The Manx Novelist', though his reputation among literary critics was, and still is, less secure. Following in his tradition the Manx author Catherine Dodd wrote thirteen historical romances, three of which were set in the Island and published in the 1920s, while Harold Blundell, writing as George Bellairs, produced several detective stories in the 1950s featuring Manx murders solved by the fictitious sleuth Archdeacon Kinrade. The most influential Manx poet of the twentieth century was probably Josephine Kermode (1852-1937), the sister of Philip, whose gentle poems about the Island and its fairy folk, written under the pen-name 'Cushag', were mostly published between 1907 and 1919.

In 1911 Sophia Morrison of Peel, a lifelong promoter of Manx and Celtic culture, published her collection entitled 'Manx Fairy Tales' and a later edition in 1929 was illustrated by Archibald Knox (1864-1933). Born and educated on the Island Knox taught at the Douglas School of Art and between 1897 and 1912 worked for Liberty's in London designing pewter and silver articles in an Art Nouveau style

The Villa Marina, Douglas. (Miles Cowsill)

which featured the interlace designs of the Manx crosses. John Miller Nicholson (1840-1913) was a successful Manx painter, as was his grandson John Hobson Nicholson (1911-1988), joining E.C.Quayle, J.H.Butterworth, John Holland, Peter Chisholm, Frederick Leach and others. William Hoggatt (1879-1961), though not Manx, settled on the Island in 1906 and painted many fine pictures of the landscape.

Music, especially singing and dance, has always been popular on the Island. In 1799 a collection of hymns in Manx was published and music was strong in the churches during the nineteenth century, especially when played by the 'West Gallery' groups who specialized in instrumental pieces in the style of Purcell or Handel, some of them composed on the Island. Manx carvals, a sort of carol, were popular during the eighteenth and nineteenth centuries and were performed by singers who started at the west end of the church and took a step forward towards the communion rail at the beginning of each verse, telling the chosen story (the Prodigal Son was a favourite) as they went. In 1892 the Manx Music Festival (known as 'The Guild') was founded and has ever since continued to provide keenly contested competitions for amateur singers from the Island.

In 1896 William Gill compiled his 'Manx National Song Book' and during the twentieth century the haunting Manx air 'Ellan Vannin' became extremely popular. In 1998 it was given global circulation in a 'pop' version sung by the Manx-born brothers Gibb, otherwise known as the Bee Gees. However, the Manx National Anthem is 'O Land of our Birth', the words written by Gill and the music adapted by him from 'Mylecharaine', which had become one of the most popular tunes in the Island by the nineteenth century. It is not easy to write acceptable words for any country's national anthem, but Gill did well:

> O Land of our birth
> O gem of God's earth,
> O Island so strong and so fair;
> Built firm as Barrule
> Thy throne of Home Rule
> Makes us free as thy sweet mountain air.

In 2003 Tynwald officially designated this song as the Manx National Anthem, to be used on official and ceremonial occasions, declaring at the same time that 'God Save the Queen' should be called the Royal Anthem and should be used in addition whenever the Sovereign, members of the Royal Family, or the Lieutenant Governor are present. The main venues for musical events in the twentieth century and since have been the Villa Marina and the Gaiety Theatre in Douglas as well as the Port Erin Arts Centre, set up in the 1980s, which presents an ambitious programme of classical concerts and recitals. In 1977 there was a revival of Yn Chruinnaght, the Manx Gaelic Festival, which encouraged a considerable number of local artists to perform and record traditional songs.

During the 1960s and 1970s the Island became well known for maintaining the controversial practice of administering judicial corporal punishment with the birch. The UK abolished this in 1948 but it was retained in the Island and until 1960 it was used about seven times a year to punish boys under 15 found guilty of petty larceny. In 1960 Tynwald decided to raise the eligible age for corporal punishment from 15 to 21, stipulating that boys under 14 should be caned over their trousers and youths up to 21 should receive the birch on their bare buttocks. During the 1960s only 18 boys under 14 were caned and the practice lapsed in 1971 but between 1960 and 1976 some 60 young men were birched. During the 1960s when the UK seaside resorts were plagued by hooligans such as 'mods and rockers' the Island's authorities argued that the birching policy (often used against violent young holidaymakers) made it seem a safer place, and most Manx people supported it.

However, an anti-birching movement led by three determined women on the Island gathered momentum and in 1972 a Manx schoolboy who had been sentenced to birching for assaulting a prefect at his school was the first person to appeal against the sentence. The Manx courts rejected the appeal and the boy was birched several weeks after the offence but backed by the anti-birching lobby he then appealed to the European Court of Human Rights. Meanwhile the controversy was given a great deal of coverage in the UK and Manx newspapers with most public opinion on the Island continuing to favour the birch. After long delays the Court of Human Rights decided in 1978 by six votes to one that birching was a degrading punishment and left the UK (which was a signatory to the 1952 Convention which set up the Court) to implement the decision. Given the Island's unique constitutional relationship with the UK, this caused difficulties.

In fact the legislation remained in force and in 1981 a Manx magistrate again sentenced a boy to be birched. This time the boy's appeal was upheld in the Manx Courts and no-one has been birched since. The legislation was repealed in 1993 and one of the arguments used in favour of repeal was that if someone was sentenced to be birched the likelihood would be that he and his family would make a great deal of money by selling their story to the newspapers. The Manx inclination to be conservative and also a touch puritanical was further highlighted by the reluctance of Tynwald to follow the UK in its 1967 decriminalization of homosexuality and it was not until 1991 that the House of Keys, after heavy pressure from the Home Office, passed the necessary legislation by 13 votes to 11. Both these controversies, though very fiery at the time, rapidly ceased to be significant issues once the critical decisions were taken and stereotypical castings of the Manx as a homophobic 'hang-em and flog-em' brigade are as out-of-date as the earlier popular notions that they were a nest of smugglers or a community of drunkards clinging to a rock in the Irish Sea.

One of the great popular survivals in the Island, though again not without controversy, has been the TT races, which celebrated their centenary in 2007. These started again after the war in 1947 and in

The Steve Hislop Garden, Onchan, overlooking Douglas, placed first in a list of the top ten seaside towns in the British Isles by 'The Times' on-line in 2007. (Miles Cowsill)

1956 they became part of the World Championship series of races, a notable achievement for the Island. During the 1960s Japanese machines began to make their presence felt and by the 1970s technological improvements led to record speeds. Before 1939 the fastest laps of the course, consisting of thirty-seven and three-quarter miles (60.75kms) of very ordinary suburban, country and mountain road with plenty of tight bends, were under 90mph but by 1970 they had reached 105mph and have subsequently climbed to well over 120mph. As a result the toll of deaths and serious injuries among participants and onlookers has been significant. In 1972 there were protests from some leading international riders and in 1989 the TT was removed from the World Championship series. To compensate for this the event was turned into a two-week festival which attracted some 40,000 visitors and 15,000 motorcycles to the Island. In 1994 there were 620 entries in the eight events on offer from 572 competitors from 20 countries.

A chief feature of the festival has been 'Mad Sunday' when the course was open to thousands of bikers, many of them foreigners used to driving on the right, and mayhem frequently ensued, along with casualties. The UK and international press took an increasingly hostile stance to the TT and in 1996 the *Daily Telegraph* reported that in 1995 there had been 1,550 hospital attendances as a result of the TT fortnight and that on 'Mad Sunday' in 1996 twelve bikers had been admitted to hospital and 25 bikes badly damaged. Moreover, several deaths each year, either in the races or the practices, were to be expected. Despite all this, public opinion on the Island generally supported the races though some people found the road closures a serious nuisance. Defenders of the races pointed out that the casualties were not excessive given the number of motorcyclists on the roads during the festival, and that the bikers themselves were well aware of the risks. In 2007 the centenary of the TT races was celebrated in fine style, attracting some 20,000 bikes and 46,000 visitors to the Island, where the Peel Bay Festival staged a series of high-profile pop concerts in what was claimed to be the largest marquee in the British Isles.

The great names of the TT have developed a cult following over the years, with Geoff Duke, Mike Hailwood, Steve Hislop, Joey Dunlop and Carl Fogarty notable among them and a charming Garden of Remembrance featuring a statue of Steve Hislop was opened on a stunning site on Onchan Head in 2005. Manx Radio offered specialist coverage of the TT races from 1987 onwards and generally developed as the Island's national radio station while also managing to reach the coastal fringes of the Irish Sea. It provided light music entertainment with commercial breaks and used its subsidy from Tynwald to broadcast current affairs and magazine programmes, claiming to reach about 80% of the Manx population. It beat off a Tynwald scheme to sell it to an entrepreneur in the 1990s but has since faced lively competition from Energy FM and 3FM, established on the Island since 2002 .

The first Manx newspaper was the *Manks Mercury*, published in 1792, followed by the *Manks Advertiser* in 1801 and they mostly provided international news for the benefit of non-Manx residents. The *Manx Sun* had its origins in 1821 and the *Mona's Herald* in 1833, both pursuing a political agenda, and the *Isle of Man Times* appeared in 1847. This was taken over in 1861 by the businessman and printer James Brown who campaigned for a reformed House of Keys and, as we have seen, was scandalously imprisoned by the House for contempt. In 1880 the *Isle of Man Examiner* first appeared, as a supporter of Nonconformists and trade unionists. From 1884 the *Times* got the contract to provide official reports of Tynwald and in 1897 the first Manx daily appeared, the *Daily Times*, and prospered

Horse Tram on the Promenade, Douglas. (Miles Cowsill)

until the UK newspapers began to be flown in to the Island on a regular basis in the 1930s.

As a result of vigorous marketing and the introduction of new production technologies, the *Examiner* had the biggest circulation by 1938 and in 1958 its owner took over the *Times* and reduced daily production to a weekly one in 1966 because it was more profitable. The Examiner Group was challenged in the 1970s by the *Isle of Man Courier* and the *Mona's Herald* closed in 1975 after an industrial dispute. Further disputes over the introduction of computer technology closed the Examiner Group itself in 1987 and former members of its staff launched the *Manx Independent*. The Examiner Group's assets were bought by the *Courier*, which had been a free-sheet since 1982, and it also acquired the *Independent*. Since then 'Isle of Man Newspapers' has been responsible for publishing the Island's three main weekly papers to a high standard.

The Island also has its own currency and stamps. The earliest Manx coins may well have been Hiberno-Norse examples such as those found in the Kirk Michael hoards discovered in 1972 and 1975, dating from the early part of the 11th century. Manx coins were made in 1668 by John Mursey, a Douglas merchant, and were legalized by

A selection of Manx currency . (DOT&L)

'Ben-my-Chree' (6). (Miles Cowsill)

Tynwald. In 1709 an issue of Manx copper pence and half pence was authorized, followed by another in 1758. George III coins were minted in 1786 and large cartwheel coins were issued in 1798 and 1813. The first Queen Victoria coins appeared in 1839, followed by successive issues up to 1971 when coins of decimal value were produced, including a pound coin in 1978. Banknotes were issued from the eighteenth century onwards by Island banks but in 1961 Tynwald revoked all existing licences to issue banknotes and since then the Isle of Man Bank has managed the note issue on behalf of the Government. In 1983 one pound plastic notes appeared as an experiment but they were replaced with paper ones in 1988. Aware that it could provide a useful source of revenue for the Island, the Manx Government set up its own independent postal administration in 1973 and since that date many different artists have designed successive issues of attractive and colourful stamps which must be used for items posted in the Island.

The changing nature of the Manx economy and in particular the decline of the holiday trade from the 1980s onwards had important repercussions for the Island's transport links. In 1962 the Steam Packet invested in a purpose-built car ferry, the *Manx Maid*, equipped with a spiral loading ramp suitable for the harbour facilities at Liverpool and Douglas. Three sister ferries, the *Ben-my-Chree, Mona's*

TT Races 2007. (Miles Cowsill)

Queen and *Lady of Mann* followed in 1966, 1972 and 1976. In 1978 a new rival company called Manx Line built a linkspan in Douglas harbour and operated a roll-on, roll-off service to Heysham. The two companies merged under the Steam Packet name in 1985 and Douglas to Heysham became the main route, with Liverpool being used during the summer season. Competition from air transport was fierce and by 1993 only 233,633 passengers arrived by sea compared with 257,357 by air. In 1998 The Steam Packet commissioned its biggest ship so far, a large roll-on roll-off ferry named the *Ben-my-Chree* which worked the Douglas to Heysham route and provided space for a large number of container lorries though - controversially at first - it had less space than its predecessors for passengers. The Liverpool route was worked by two fast vessels, with the *Lady of Mann* retained until 2005 for seasonal work. During the summer the fast craft and the *Lady of Mann* also ran services to Dublin and Belfast. After the 'Lady' was decommissioned the Steam Packet fleet consisted of just two vessels but between them they were able to provide the necessary transport links for cargo and passengers.

Andreas airfield ceased to operate in 1946 and Jurby in 1963 but

Ronaldsway has steadily been improved and enlarged. A new terminal building was completed in 1953 and in 1973 there were a record 480,000 arrivals and departures. Then followed a marked fall down to 283,000 in 1982 because of the international oil crisis and the decline of the holiday industry but the development of the financial sector led to the foundation of Manx Airlines in 1982 and by 1987 425,000 passengers passed through Ronaldsway. The airport buildings were greatly enlarged and improved in the 1990s and a freeport was established nearby, while Manx Airlines was taken over for a time by British Airways which in turn sold on to other operators. The number of passengers using the airport grew from 600,000 in 1996 to nearly 774,000 in 2004 and successive airline companies have operated routes to London, Dublin, Liverpool, Luton, Manchester, Birmingham, Bristol, Newcastle, Southampton, Glasgow and Blackpool as well as other destinations. The Island's 'new tourism' is not of the former bucket-and-spade variety but relies upon short stays, upgraded hotels, expanded self-catering provision and clients of the finance and film industries.

No longer can it be said that the Island of Manannan mac Lir lies remote and mysterious beyond some fabled horizon. During the

Tynwald Day 2007. (Miles Cowsill)

The Isle of Man's Coat-of-Arms, displayed on the Government Buildings in Douglas. (Miles Cowsill)

twentieth century it became familiar to millions of British holidaymakers and in the last few decades it has emerged as a serious player in the world of international finance. In the twenty-first century the Isle of Man is a self-governing Crown Dependency outside both the United Kingdom and the European Union, identifiably British, but also proudly Manx. It remains significantly different from the rest of the British Isles, with its own parliament, language, laws, currency, stamps and tax structure as well as its TT races, tailless Manx cats, many-horned loaghtan sheep and unique railway system. Tynwald announced in 2006 that its strategy was to promote the Island's 'Freedom to Flourish', affirming that it is 'a land of opportunity where people and business will find the right environment in which to reach their full potential, whatever they feel that might be'. Promotion of the Island's successful economy is a major priority of the Manx Government, together with the nourishing of its national identity and heritage. This is as it should be, for few places so small have so rich a story to tell.

Appendix

THE THREE LEGS OF MAN

The earliest examples of the 'triskele', probably a sun-symbol, come from Sicily at the end of the seventh century BC and since then it has been used as an emblem in that three-cornered island. It also appears on Greek coins from the sixth century BC onwards. A triple-knot design, incorporating the three legs symbol, was used on a silver penny issued about 941 AD by Anlaf Cuaran, the Norse king of Dublin and York, who is very likely to have ruled over the Isle of Man at some period in the mid-tenth century. The Rolls of Arms, which are the oldest English heraldic manuscripts, reveal that the shield technically described as 'Gules three legs in armour argent' (three silver armoured legs on a red background) was firmly associated with the Kings of Man during the thirteenth century. Moreover Segar's Roll (c 1280) provides a clear drawing of the three legs, armed in chain mail, and a similar design was much used by Alexander III of Scotland after he became King of Man in 1266. The earliest known representation of the device on the Island, featuring the legs clad in plate armour, was carved on a stone cross found at Maughold and it is thought to be from the period of the Montacute kings (1333-1391). It also appears on the Manx Sword of State which, according to the most recent research, dates from the fifteenth century rather than an earlier period. Since then the triskele has steadily become the predominant emblem of the Island. In 1932 the UK Government sanctioned its use on the Island's national flag and in 1996 it became the centrepiece of a new Coat-of-Arms granted to the Island by Royal Warrant. The three legs are supported by a peregrine falcon, referring to Henry IV's grant of the Island to Sir John Stanley in return for the gift of two falcons to him and to every future sovereign of England on their Coronation Day, and a raven because Odin, the Norse God, was generally described as being accompanied by two ravens. The origin of the motto 'Quocunque Jeceris Stabit' (wherever you throw it, it will stand) is not known for certain, but it might derive from a witticism of King James I who made the remark about his canny Lord Chief Justice, Sir Edward Coke. The motto's earliest known use on the Island was on penny coins issued in 1668.

Sources

PRIMARY

Broderick, George, (editor and translator) *Chronicles of the Kings of Man and the Isles*, Manx National Heritage, Douglas, 1996.

GENERAL HISTORIES

Belchem, John, (ed.) *The Modern Period, 1830-1999*, A New History of the Isle of Man, Volume 5, Liverpool University Press, 2000.

Chiverrell, Richard, and Thomas, Geoffrey, (eds) *The Evolution of the Natural Landscape*, A New History of the Isle of Man, Volume 1, Liverpool University Press, 2006.

Duffy, E., (ed.) *The Mediaeval Period, 1000-1405*, A New History of the Isle of Man, Volume 3, Liverpool University Press, expected in 2007/08.

Kinvig, R.H., *The Isle of Man, A Social, Cultural and Political History*, Liverpool University Press, third edition, 1975.

Moore, A.W., *A History of the Isle of Man*, (two vols) Fisher Unwin, London 1900.

Stenning, E.W., *Portrait of the Isle of Man*, Robert Hale, London, 1965.

SPECIALIST STUDIES

'IOMNHAS' denotes the 'Proceedings of the Isle of Man Natural History and Antiquarian Society'.

Bagley, J.J., *The Earls of Derby, 1485-1985*, Sidgwick and Jackson, London 1985.

Broderick, George, *A Dictionary of Manx Place-Names*, English Place-Name Society, Nottingham, 2006.

Caine, P.W., *The Bishop of the Manx Bible*, IOMNHAS Vol IV.
The Story of the House of Keys, IOMNHAS Vol IV, No4

Cresswell, Yvonne (ed.) *Living with the Wire*, Manx National Heritage pamphlet, 1994.

Cowsill, Miles, and Hendy, John (eds) *Steam Packet 175*, Ferry Publications, Ramsey, 2005

Cubbon, A.M., *The Art of the Manx Crosses*, Manx National Heritage pamphlet, third edition, 1983.
P.M.C.Kermode, An Appreciation on the Centenary of the Manx Museum, IOMNHAS Vol IX, No3

Cubbon, A.M., and others, *Prehistoric Sites in the Isle of Man*. Manx National Heritage pamphlet, revised edition, 2005.

Curphey, R.A., *The Background to the Disputed Derby Succession*, IOMNHAS Vol VII

Peel Castle, IOMNHAS, Vol IX, No1

Davey, P.R., *An Overview of the archaeology of the Isle of Man* (Draft ms)

Dickinson, J.R., *The Lordship of Man under the Stanleys*, Centre for Manx Studies, Douglas, 1997

Eliza Endangered? Elizabeth I, the Isle of Man and the Security of England, IOMNHAS Vol X, No 1

Dugdale, D.S., *Manx Church Origins*, Llanerch, 1998.

Fellows-Jensen, Gillian, *How Old are the Scandinavian Place-Names in Man?* IOMNHAS Vol XI No2

Ferry, Fergus, *A Guide to Early Irish Law*, Dublin Institute for Advanced Studies, 1988, 2005 reprint.

Early Irish Farming, Dublin Institute for Advanced Studies, 1997.

Garrad, L.S., and others, *The Industrial Archaeology of the Isle of Man*, David and Charles, Newton Abbot, 1972.

Gelling, John, *A History of the Manx Church, 1698-1911*, The Manx Heritage Foundation, 1998.

Isle of Man Treasury, *Isle of Man National Income, 2004/2005*, (pamphlet).

James, Simon, *The Atlantic Celts*, British Museum Press, 1999

Kermode, David G., *Offshore Island Politics*, Liverpool Univ. Press, 2001.

Kermode, P.M.C., *Manx Crosses*, 1907

Kewley Draskau, Jennifer (ed. and transl.) *Account of the Isle of Man in Song*, Centre for Manx Studies Monograph 5, 2006

Kneale, Peter, *90 Years of TT Magic*, The Manx Experience, Douglas, 1998.

Kniveton, Gordon, *The Isle of Man Steam Railway*, The Manx Experience, Douglas, revised edition, 1993.

MacInnes, A.I., *Scotland and the Manx Connection: Relationships of Intermittent Violence, 1266c-1606*, IOMNHAS Vol VIII

McDonald, R.Andrew, *Manx Kingship in its Irish Sea Setting, 1187-1229*, Four Courts Press, Dublin 2007.

Norris, Samuel, *Manx Memories and Movements*, 1938, MHF reprint, 1994.

Raftery, Barry, *Pagan Celtic Ireland*, Thames and Hudson, 1994

Richards, Julian D., *Viking Age England*, Batsford, 1991

Robinson, Vaughan, and McCarroll, Danny, *The Isle of Man, Celebrating a Sense of Place*, Liverpool University Press 1990.

Stott, Ros, *A Brief Encounter, The Duke of Atholl and the Isle of Man 1736-1764*, in Davey, Peter, and Finlayson, David (eds), *Mannin Revisited*, Scottish Society for Northern Studies, 2002

Thomson, R.L., and Pilgrim, A.J., *Outline of Manx Language and Literature*, Yn Cheshaght Ghailckagh pamphlet, no date.

Waddell, John, *The Prehistoric Archaeology of Ireland*, Wordwell, 2000

West, J.I. *John Wesley in the Isle of Man*, IOMNHAS Vol VI.
Sir Thomas Fairfax and the Isle of Man, IOMNHAS Vol VI.

Whitney, J.T. *Isle of Man Stamps and Postal History*, BPH Publications, 1981

Wilkins, Frances, *The Isle of Man in Smuggling History*, Wyre Forest Press 1992.

Wilson, D.M., *The Chronology of the Viking Age in the Isle of Man*, IOMNHAS Vol X No 4

Wilson, R.J.A., *On the Trail of the Triskeles*, Cambridge Archaeological Journal, Vol 10, No 1, 2000

Winterbottom, Derek, *T.E.Brown, His Life and Legacy*, Manx Experience, 1997.
Governors of the Isle of Man since 1765, Manx Heritage Foundation, 1999.
Economic History 1830-1996, in Belchem, John (ed) A New History of the Isle of Man, Vol 5, Liverpool University Press, 2000.
Charles Kerruish, Manx Politician and Parliamentarian, MHF, 2000.
The Story of Manx Radio, 1964-2004, Manx Experience, 2004.
Henry Bloom Noble, His Life and the work of his Trust, MHF, 2005.

The Oxford Dictionary of National Biography, (OUP, 2004), entries by:

Bennett, Michael J., *Sir John Stanley*
Thomas, first Baron Stanley

Callow, John, *Charlotte, Countess of Derby*

Coward, Barry, *James Stanley, seventh Earl of Derby*

Dickinson, J.R., *William Christian*

Gentles, Ian J, *Thomas Fairfax*

Kathman, David, *Ferdinando Stanley, fifth Earl of Derby*

Knafla, Louis A., *Edward Stanley, third Earl of Derby*
Henry Stanley, fourth Earl of Derby

Lassiter, J.C., *James Stanley, tenth Earl of Derby*

Mason, J.J., *Robert Duckenfield*

Rapple, Rory, *Thomas Stanley, first Earl of Derby*

Troxler, Carol Watterson, *Thomas Wilson*

Williams, N.J.A., *Mark Hildesley*

Kings and Lords of Man

THE SCANDINAVIAN KINGS OF MAN AND THE ISLES

Between c 900 and 1079 AD it is very likely that there were successive kings of Norse origin ruling in Man but we do not know their names and dates for certain.

1079-1095	Godred Crovan
1095-1113	period of unrest, dominated by Magnus, King of Norway
1113-1153	Olaf I
1153-1187	Godred II
1187-1228	Reginald I
1228-1237	Olaf II
1237-1248	Harald I
1249	Reginald II
1252-1265	Magnus

SCOTTISH AND ENGLISH RULE

1266-1284	Alexander III of Scotland
1290-1293	Edward I of England
1293-1296	John Balliol, King of Scotland
1301-1311	Anthony Bek, Bishop of Durham
1311	Piers Gaveston
1312-1313	Henry de Beaumont
1313-1316	Robert I, King of Scotland
1316-1332	Thomas, Earl of Moray
1333-1344	William de Montacute I, Earl of Salisbury
1344-1392	William de Montacute II, Earl of Salisbury
1392-1399	William le Scrope, Earl of Wiltshire
1399-1405	Henry Percy, Earl of Northumberland

THE STANLEYS

1406	Sir John Stanley I
1414	Sir John Stanley II
1437	Thomas, first Lord Stanley
1460	Thomas, first Earl of Derby
1504	Thomas, second Earl, preferred the title 'Lord of Man' to King'
1521	Edward, third Earl
1572	Henry, fourth Earl
1593	Ferdinando, fifth Earl

1594	Queen Elizabeth I
1603	King James I
1612	William, sixth Earl and his wife Elizabeth
1642	James, seventh Earl
1651	Thomas, Lord Fairfax
1660	Charles, eighth Earl
1672	William, ninth Earl
1702	James, tenth Earl

THE ATHOLLS

1736	James Murray, second Duke of Atholl
1764	John Murray, third Duke, in right of his wife Charlotte

UK SOVEREIGNS SINCE REVESTMENT

1765	George III
1820	George IV
1830	William IV
1837	Victoria
1901	Edward VII
1910	George V
1936	Edward VIII
1936	George VI
1952	Elizabeth II

GOVERNORS OF THE ISLAND SINCE 1406

The Kings of Man before 1406 no doubt appointed governors to carry out the administration of the Island in their absence, but information about them is patchy, while the records from 1406 are much more reliable (though not completely). Between 1406 and 1652 the title was usually Governor or Captain, between 1652 and 1830 Governor, and since then it has been Lieutenant Governor.

1406 Michael Blundell	1690 Roger Kenyon
1417 John Litherland	1693 William Sacheverell
1422 John Walton	1696 Col Nicholas Sankey
1428 Henry Byron	1701 James Cranstown
1496 Peter Dutton	1702 Hon. Charles Stanley
1497 Abbot Henry Radcliffe	1703 Robert Mawdesley
1508 Ralph Rushton	1713 Hon. Charles Z. Stanley
1511 Sir John Ireland	1718 Alexander Horne
1518 John Ffasakerly	1723 John Lloyd
1521 Thomas Danport	1725 Thomas Horton
1527 Henry Stanley	1736 James Murray
1532 John Ffleming	1744 Patrick Lindesay
1536 George Stanley	1751 Basil Cochrane
1545 William Stanley	1761 John Wood
1552 Henry Stanley	1777 Major-Gen. Edward Smith
1570 Henry Tarbock	1793 John Murray, fourth Duke of Atholl
1576 John Harmer	1830 Col Cornelius Smelt
1580 Richard Sherburne	1832 Major-Gen. John Ready
Bishop John Meyrick	1845 Hon. Charles Hope
1592 Cuthbert Gerard	1860 Francis Stainsby-Conant-Pigott
1593 Hon. William Stanley	1863 Sir Henry Loch
1594 Randulph Stanley	1882 Sir Spencer Walpole
1595 Sir Thomas Gerard	1893 Sir Joseph Ridgeway
1596 Peter Legh	1895 John Henniker-Major, fourth Baron
1599 Cuthbert Gerard	Henniker
1600 Robert Molynieux	1902 George Somerset, third Baron Raglan
1609 John Ireland	1919 Major-Gen. Sir William Fry
1623 Sir Frederick Liege	1926 Sir Claude Hill
1626 Edward Holmewood	1933 Sir Montagu Butler
1627 Sir Charles Gerrard	1937 Vice-Admiral William Leveson-
1628 Edward Christian	Gower, fourth Earl Granville
1639 Ffoulkes Hunckes	1945 Air Vice-Marshal Sir Geoffrey Bromet
1640 John Greenhalghe	1952 Sir Ambrose Flux Dundas
1651 Sir Philip Musgrave	1959 Sir Ronald Garvey
1651 Col. Robert Duckenfield	1966 Sir Peter Stallard
1652 Matthew Cadwell	1974 Sir John Paul
1656 William Christian	1980 Rear-Admiral Sir Nigel Cecil
1659 James Chaloner	1985 Major-Gen. Sir Laurence New
1660 Roger Nowell	1990 Air Marshal Sir Laurence Jones
1664 Bishop Isaac Barrow	1995 Sir Timothy Daunt
1673 Henry Nowell	2000 Air Marshal Ian Macfadyen
1677 Henry Stanley	2005 Vice-Admiral Sir Paul Haddacks
1678 Robert Heywood	

INDEX